To   My   Mother

ACKNOWLEDGEMENTS

I wish to express my deep gratitude to my advisor, Dr. Sham Navathe, for his insightful critique and perspicacious guidance in the course of this work. Over the long years of our association, I came to highly value his friendship, consul and erudition. I indeed owe him a great deal.

I am indebted to my supervisory committee members, Dr. Stanley Su, Dr. Ravi Varadarajan, Dr. Prabhat Hajela, Dr. Sharma Chakravarthy and Dr. Herman Lam for their time, patience and helpful suggestions.

My sincerest thanks go to Dr. Daniel Fishman of Hewlett-Packard Laboratories for his constant encouragement and support. This research was partially funded with a grant made by him.

I greatly appreciate the unceasing help and assistance provided by Mrs. Sharon Grant.

As I prepare to bid farewell to my alma mater, I would like to take this opportunity to thank all those unnamed friends and associates, who contributed in creating a climate conducive to my academic and nonacademic pursuits.

TABLE OF CONTENTS

Abstract of Dissertation Presented to the Graduate School
of the University of Florida in Partial Fulfillment of the
Requirements for the Degree of Doctor of Philosophy

VERSION CONTROL AND MANAGEMENT IN COMPUTER-AIDED
DESIGN DATABASES

By

Rafi Ahmed

December 1989

Chairman: Dr. Shamkant B. Navathe
Major Department: Computer and Information Sciences

There are essentially two characteristics of design objects which impact upon the iterative and probative nature of the design process. First, they are hierarchically formed assemblies of component objects. Second, they have several alternative representations. This dissertation addresses a broad spectrum of modeling and operational issues related to these two aspects in computer-aided design databases.

A formal treatment of data modeling concepts, which are defined in terms of primitive constructs of instances, types, homogeneous sets and functions, and abstractions of generalization and composition, is presented for design applications.

A classification of composite object attributes into intrinsic interface and extrinsic internal assembly provides an insight into their behavior and functionality. The design process is studied with respect to these classes of attributes. A design evolves in discrete states through mutation and derivation, which may cause version

vi

proliferation in the absence of any control mechanism. Concepts of invariant attributes and value acquisition are found to be useful for developing a notion of version equivalence. A wide range of methodologies for version management and solutions for the related problems are discussed.

The interdependence between composition and generalization graphs suggests that the effect of updates in these graphs on each other must be evaluated for maintaining consistency. A time complexity analysis of algorithms devised for this purpose shows a considerably improved performance when the stored, rather than the dynamically computed, transitive closures of these graphs are used. The trade-off it provides far outweighs the space requirement of the transitive closure relations.

Owing to the sheer complexity and size of design databases, efficient organization and access of versioned composite objects become imperative. The proposed scheme and its related algorithms can determine an optimal storage organization based on significant units of clustering and expected frequency of retrieval and update operations.

A multi-layer architecture is motivated by the accessibility and stability of versions they contain. The proposed protocols for sharing and transition of versions together with change notification provide a unifying framework for managing design in a cooperative CAD environment.

CHAPTER 1
INTRODUCTION

1.1 Preliminary Discussion

In recent years, there has been a tremendous surge of interest in the research and development of computer-aided design (CAD) systems for aiding and controlling the design efforts of a wide variety of engineering products, including VLSI circuits, mechanical parts, software systems, etc. The size and complexity of many design projects have rendered existing database tools and support inadequate. Database systems designed for commercial applications suffer from the fact that they normally hold only one valid view of the world. In integrated CAD systems, designers often need to generate and experiment with multiple alternative representations of an object before selecting one that meets the design requirements. This means that several valid representations of an object may coexist in the database. Furthermore, a traditional database system, as it deals with only regular and structured data, cannot efficiently manage design data, which are often hierarchical in nature and entail large variations in their size and structure. In order to support the varied requirements, we need a unified system which incorporates these concepts and provides tools for an efficient management of a generalized design database.

Design of an object normally starts with a high level description of some aspects of that object. Because of the iterative nature of the design process, a complete description of the design cannot be provided at once; only a partial description is provided which is later completed by repeated refinements. Because of the probative nature of the design process, in each step of the iteration, several admissible alternatives may exist. Designers usually choose one alternative and proceed to

1

finalize the design. If that alternative turns out to be inappropriate, they back up and pursue another alternative.

The iterative and probative nature of the design process interacts with two dimensions of design objects. First, they are usually complex; that is, they are assemblies of parts that themselves may be constructed hierarchically from component objects. Second, there can be several concurrent descriptions, called versions, of design objects. The problem of managing a design is compounded by the fact that composite objects can have multiple alternative configurations, if versions of components are taken into consideration. Further, creation of versions can take place either at the template— a type and a collection of attributes defined on it—level or at the instance level. The derivation sequence of versions must be represented explicitly to maintain a true version history. These characteristics must be taken into account for any systematic and efficient management of design and versioning of composite objects. The sheer size and complexity of versioned composite objects also require an efficient organization and retrieval strategy.

Management of design data in the presence of alternatives and assembly is an intricate task, which cannot be carried out efficiently with ad hoc approaches. This proposal addresses a wide range of related problems and provides a well-defined formalism and systematic methodology needed for this purpose.

1.2 The Outline

This dissertation is primarily concerned with the management of computer-aided design databases and addresses the following issues:

1. Supporting the data modeling requirements of a design database through a set of formally defined modeling constructs.

2. Developing an abstraction for composite objects based on the categorization of their attributes.

3. Proposing a mechanism for the management and control of versions for design databases.

4. Maintaining a consistent semantics of schema as the composition and generalization graphs interact with each other.

5. Proposing an efficient strategy for organizing and retrieving versioned composite objects.

6. Proposing a cooperative environment and describing protocols for efficiently managing a complex design, which is collectively developed by a group of designers working on different projects.

The remainder of the dissertation is organized as follows. In Section 1.3, the work related to this research is reviewed. The formal treatment of the proposed data modeling constructs are presented in Chapter 2. In Chapter 3, the abstraction developed for a complex design object is discussed. Chapter 4 deals with the basic modeling constructs, constraints and rules for managing version control. Then in Chapter 5, the interaction between composition and generalization graphs are investigated; an analysis of algorithms for maintaining consistent semantics and querying these constructs are presented for the case when the transitive closure is maintained vis-a-vis and when its dynamically computed. A clustering storage strategy is presented for the efficient organization and retrieval of versioned composite objects in Chapter 6. In Chapter 7, a cooperative CAD architecture is proposed to deal with a collective design effort made by a group of designers working on different projects. And finally in Chapter 8, the main results of this work are summarized and the directions for the future research in this area are indicated.

1.3 Review of Related Work

Many recent investigators have recognized the need of database technology in the CAD applications. The organizations using commercially available conventional database management systems have encountered difficulties because conventional databases do not have features to deal with unstructured data and different versions or alternatives of a design, which are required in CAD applications [Got86]. There are essentially three different solutions to these problems:

1. Extending the conventional DBMS by adding new capabilities.
2. Building a layer of software on top of conventional DBMSs to provide the required features.
3. Developing new database management systems for design applications, which involves the development of a new data model, new architecture storage strategy and enhanced facilities.

Some of the examples of the first approach were based on the enhancement of existing systems. Lori [Lor82] discusses the extensions of system R and Stonebraker et al. [Sto83] report on the enhancements of INGRES. This approach requires too extensive an enhancement to make it feasible. Some researchers provide examples of the second approach, which has some drawbacks [Joh83, Emo83]. The conventional DBMS's perform poorly in design applications, as they require another level of transformations for retrieval and manipulation of data. The extensions or modification of global schema requires major changes to the system. The third approach also advocates this with several enhancements [Kat85, Kla86, Kim87].

1.3.1 Treatment of Complex Object and Extension of DBMSs

Several investigators have observed the importance of the concept of composite objects in CAD databases, and the deficiencies of current databases in supporting them. Batory and Buchmann [Bat84] call composite objects "molecular objects," and develop a framework for modeling these objects. They introduce the notion of molecular aggregation, which is the abstraction of assemblies of parts and their relationships to higher level entities. They distinguish four different types of molecular objects, and provide methods to model objects of each type. They do not address the physical organization of the database for molecular objects.

Lorie and Plouffe [Lor83] discuss an implementation for objects, which they call "complex objects". Their central idea is to use internal fields in order to make the system aware of the hierarchical structure of objects, which allows the system to operate on a collection of tuples that represents a composite object as a unit. This idea has been extended by Meier and Lorie through the concepts of surrogates and implicit hierarchical joins [Mei83]. The implementation suggested in this work simplifies some important operations that are performed on a composite object as a whole. As a matter of fact, in their scheme, the whole design database is about one object, but designers manipulate only the portions of the design object at each stage of design; therefore, only some of the data that describes the design needs to be accessed.

Wiederhold et al. address the problem of communication within a VLSI design and its different representations and hierarchical levels in a multiple designer environment using commercial database systems [Wie82]. They describe some initial results of an ongoing project.

Johnson and Schweitzer provide facilities to treat composite objects as single entities that they call "structure" [Joh83]. They propose a three-level modeling approach. The internal level is based on the network data model. The mapping from logical level to interval level is defined by database designers. The mapping from the internal level to the physical level is provided by the system.

Emond and Merechal use the ER approach to model composite object at the logical level [Emo83]. These models are then translated by the designer into a relational database. In this work, information is divided into blocks called "view-editions", which are the units of storage retrieval and update operations.

Stonebraker et al. introduce user-defined ADT's (Abstract Data Types) and ADT indices to relational DBMS INGRES for supporting representation and retrieval of composite objects [Sto83]. The use of ADT simplifies the definition and logical manipulation of composite objects by allowing user defined data types and operations on these types.

Su et al. propose an object-oriented semantic association model called OSAM* [Su88]. OSAM* has powerful expressive capabilities, as it supports constructors in nested and recursive fashions to represent complex and composite objects.

Batory and Kim propose modeling concepts for VLSI objects [Bat85]. They use entity-relationship diagram to represent these objects which has interface descriptions and implementation descriptions. A molecular object is created by integrating these two sets of heterogeneous records. They also propose a notion of "instantiation", which are essentially copies of other objects, as they share the same features, and are needed as constituents of other objects. The modeling framework provided in this work is very useful in representing composite objects and their versions; however, it does not provide explicit support for the aggregation hierarchy.

Kim et al. discuss the facilities for the composite objects in ORION data model by introducing "is-part-of" relationship between objects [Kim89]. Composite objects in ORION are simply an aggregation hierarchy with some notions of integrity and existence dependencies. They also present some mechanisms for enhancing the performance of operational database systems by using ideas of clustering and objects as the unit of locking.

1.3.2 Version Management

The deficiencies of current DBMS's with respect to the management of refinements, alternatives and versions of designs have been recognized and discussed in the literature extensively. Most of the proposed solutions claim to be object oriented. Refinements of a design are represented as versions of design files by the subsystem called the "datamanager" [Ben82]. The datamanager manages the evolution of different versions of the file through time. A group of files can be related in content. The nature of relations are user defined and application dependent. For instance, two related files may contain a description of the two aspects of the same object; one file may also describe the component of the object represented by other file.

Eastman uses the notion of a "checkpoint" file to support refinements [Eas80]. Checkpoint files are temporary files into which a set of database updates are stored. Each checkpoint file, called an "alternative", is a refinement of the design. Multiple alternatives may be created starting from the initial design conditions. Alternatives may branch from other alternatives and thus create a tree.

Katz proposes a set of "alternatives" objects which are themselves groupings of versions [Kat82]. Alternatives have the same behavior but have differing performance characteristics. Versions are improvements or corrections applied to design objects. Representations have hierarchical structure represented as a directed acyclic graph. The leaves of this hierarchy are primitive objects, while internal nodes are complex objects. Objects are implemented as files extended with information which describes the design data structures. The subsystem responsible for the management of versions is called "library" [Rob81]. As in other proposals, a database object is a collection of data pertaining to a design object. An object may have several versions, which are of two types: in-process versions, which are mutable objects, and released objects which are immutable objects.

McLeod and Rao propose a scheme, where both refinements and alternatives are called "revisions" [McL83]. This proposal uses Tich's AND-OR graph model to abstract the state of a system at an arbitrary stage of its design. Representations are considered a kind of versions which are equivalent objects describing the same objects. This scheme requires versions to have the same external interface.

Some investigators have emphasized the multi-aspect characteristics of design objects [Neu83]. Database objects describing aspects of real world objects are called "representations". Some representations are derived from others. A derivation-graph gives type level information about which representation is derived from which. Versions are different descriptions of the object. Since representations can have several versions, there is also a version graph.

Katz et al. deal with three aspects of design: version histories, configurations, and equivalence among objects of different types [Kat86]. In this proposed design, descriptions may exist across representations. Some validation tools are discussed that provide consistency among different representations.

Landis discusses some important concepts of versioning and propagation of changes [Lan86]. Changes in this scheme can be grouped together that can postpone automatic generation of versions. This work also proposes a version graph that can have multiple successors and predecessors; two versions can also be merged into one, although no definition of "merging" is given.

Beech and Mahbod [Bee88] describe the version control facility incorporated in Iris [Fis87], an object-oriented database management system. The main features of this scheme is the treatment of generic and versioned instances of objects, facilities for explicit references and implicit coercion of references and propagation of version creation, and the use of contexts to achieve fine control in a declarative way. This paper makes a significant contribution in this area.

Navathe and Ahmed discuss the temporal semantics of version management [Nav88]. They investigate whether the work on temporal modeling bears any relationship with version control; the result of their work suggests that version management, though in need of temporal information, has significantly different requirements than that of temporal databases.

Buchmann and Celis discuss an architecture for process-plant CAD system to serve as a framework for the presentation of a data model based on the notion of molecular aggregation [Buc85]. They also suggest mechanism for constraint handling.

Chou and Kim present a model that attempts to incorporate the distributed nature of CAD environment and the complex configurations of CAD objects [Cho86]. The proposed distributed architecture has a global database that is hierarchically partioned into three different types of databases; this partitioned database interacts with three classes of versions that have different capabilities and characteristics in different databases.

1.3.3 Transitive Closure Computation

In Chapter 5, we propose maintenance and precomputation of transitive closure of type and composition graphs for their efficient processing.

The computation of transitive relationship has been recognized as a sufficiently useful operation for it to have been included in a variety of query languages. Ioannidis and Ramakrishnan present some efficient algorithms for computing the transitive closure of a directed graph [Ioa88]. They address it as a problem of reachability. They also provide an excellent comparative analysis of published algorithms in literature.

Schubert et al. proposed a technique for encoding reachability information, wherein an interval consisting of the preorder number of the node and the highest preorder number among its descendents is associated with a node [Sch83]. They also generalize their scheme to work for overlapping hierarchies.

A transitive closure technique based on chain decomposition of graphs is proposed by Jagadish [Jag88]. In this scheme, each node is indexed with a chain number and its sequence number in the chain. At each node, only the earliest node in the chain, which can be reached from it, needs to be stored. The nodes that are reachable in this chain can be deduced from this.

Agrawal et al. present transitive closure compression technique, based on labeling spanning trees with numeric intervals [Agr89]. They also provide analytical and empirical evidences of its efficiency, demonstrated by a wide range of simulation experiments and performance evaluation.

1.3.4 Storage Strategies

Schkolnick discusses the problem of storing hierarchic structure in order to minimize the expected access time [Sch77]. In it, an algorithm is presented that can determine the optimal partition of an IMS type tree into data set groups. The limitation of this work is that the instances of the given tree are assumed to be regular with same fan-out and that the partitions are stored completely independent of one another.

Carey et al. describe the file management system of the EXODUS extensible database system [Car86]. The basic abstraction in this system is the storage object, an uninterpreted variable-length record of arbitrary size. The management of large dynamic object, which can occupy many disk pages and can grow and shrink, is supported. The object is represented on disk as B+ tree index on byte position within the object plus a collection of leaf blocks containing data. As objects are primarily treated as a sequence of bytes, this technique does not appear to be suitable for storing highly structured composite and constituent objects.

Ketabchi and Berzins introduce a clustering concepts called component aggregation which considers assemblies having the same type of parts as equivalent objects [Ket88b]. They develop a mathematical model which treats equivalence classes as a form of Boolean algebra. However, the technique proposed in this work does not group objects in useful and meaningful partitions; insertion and deletion algorithms are not discussed.

Harder et al. describe the Molecule-Atom data model, aimed at the support of engineering applications [Har87]. Their database kernel provides a variety of access path structure, tuning mechanism, sort order, and some rudimentary notions of atom clustering with variable size pages and storage redundancy.

Almost all reported work that is germane to present investigation has been reviewed here. The point that emerges from the foregoing discussion is that there is a clear lack of cohesion among different schemes, and that some methodologies have been proposed without a concrete underlying data model. This dissertation addresses all aspects of this problem and provides feasible solutions within an underlying data model.

CHAPTER 2
MODELING CONSTRUCTS FOR DESIGN DATABASES

In this chapter, we *formally* define modeling constructs for design databases. These constructs are essentially based on ideas presented in existing functional, semantic and object-oriented data models. In defining these constructs, we have been particularly influenced by Iris, an object-oriented database management system [Fis87]. The discussion of these constructs is necessary, as they are used for illustrating and formalizing the concepts developed in this dissertation for the management of design databases.

The universe of discourse is viewed as a collection of objects. These objects are a convenient aggregation of information describing real world concepts. *Types, homogeneous sets, functions, user-defined instance objects*, and *literals* (to be defined shortly) are also objects. Any database conceptually contains a number of system objects, which makes it possible to define, construct and manipulate user-defined objects.

Objects of similar behavior are grouped together and are said to have the same type. Objects are instances of one or more types. Every *type* is a subtype of one or more other types, except the system-defined object, the universe of discourse, U. An instance of any type is also an instance of all its supertypes, and thus inherits a subset of the operations, functions and rules of its supertypes. A *homogeneous set* is an abstraction for a set of objects of the same type; i.e., it is a collection of either type, function, user-defined instance objects, homogeneous set, or literal objects.

2.1 The Basic Constructs

<u>Definition 2.1.</u>   Let the universe of discourse, U, be a collection of *objects*. Let the system-defined type objects T, F, UO, L and HS, which are subtypes of U, be infinite sets of *types, functions, user-defined instance objects, literals* and *homogeneous sets*, respectively, such that T, F, UO, L and HS form a partition of U.

Thus, each object o in the universe of discourse can be identified as one of the following: a type object, a function object, an instance object, a literal object, or a homogeneous set.

The subtypes of T are T_S and T_U. All user-defined types are members of T_U. All system-defined types that include U, T, F, HS, L, UO, T_U and T_S itself are members of the domain of T_S. *Boolean, real, integers* and *charstring* etc. are literals. The literal objects are always available, replicable and self-representing.

In the following definitions, we shall use the notations, $\prec$ and $\succ$ for "is a subtype of" and "is a supertype of," respectively. The symbols $\Rightarrow$, $\rightarrow$, := stand for logical implication, functional mapping, and assignment, respectively.

<u>Definition 2.2.</u>   For each type t the domain of t is represented by $dom(t)$, which is given by the set of all objects that are of type t.

For notational convenience, we shall use t (unitalicized) for the domain, $dom(t)$, of type t (italicized) interchangeably.

<u>Definition 2.3.</u>   For each type $t \in T$, there exists a system-defined unary predicate that has the same name as the associated type. This predicate is a mapping from objects in U to Boolean values, *true* and *false*.

$$\forall \ t \ \in dom(T), \quad t : U \ \rightarrow \ Boolean$$

$$\forall \ o \ \in \ dom(U), \quad t(o) \ \Longleftrightarrow \ o \ \in \ dom(t)$$

That is, every type name is also used as a predicate function in order to determine whether the given object is of that type.

UO contains all the user-defined object instances of user-defined types T_U. All literals are subtypes of L, whereas all user-defined types (i.e., instances of T_U) are subtypes of UO, which forms the root of *generalization graph* (Definition 2.6). Figure 2-1 shows this subtype/supertype relationship. Therefore, all instances of user-defined types are members of UO as well as of one or more user-defined types. Some members of UO may also be instances of some system-defined types T_S.

$$\forall \; i \in dom(UO) \;\; \exists \; t \in dom(T_U) \;\; | \;\; t \prec UO \;\wedge\; t(i) \;=\; true$$

The other essential concept is that of a function. *Functions* are named objects that take one or more arguments and return results. A function may be single-, unique-, or multi-valued, and each of its result may be a tuple of values. These functions are not strict mathematical functions, since they are not necessarily single-valued. However, they can be used to model mathematical functions by declaring them to be single-valued.

<u>Definition 2.4.</u> A function is a mapping from domains of one or more types to the domain of a list of types. A function $f \in F$ is given by

$$f \;:\; t_1, t_2, \ldots, t_i \;\rightarrow\; < t_{i+1}, \ldots, t_n >$$

$t_1, t_2, \ldots, t_i, t_{i+1} \ldots t_n \in dom(T)$, and are not necessarily distinct. That is, a function is a single- or multi-valued mapping from a set of objects to another set of objects. For notational convenience, the symbols "$<$" and "$>$" are dropped from the n-place tuple, if n is 1.

Functions can be nested to any depth, and can be defined in terms of other function(s). They are a powerful means that is used to model properties (attributes) of objects and their n-ary relationships. The set of functions defined on a type describes the behavior of objects that are instances of that type. Since functions are defined on any object type, this allows a uniform mechanism for querying user-defined data as well as meta data. The results of the collection of functions defined on an object determines the state of the object, whereas operations change the state of an object, or create and delete an object.

Creation of a homogeneous set is a mechanism that allows a collection of objects to be grouped together. A *homogeneous set* is an object which can be defined to be equivalent to either an enumerated set of objects or a set formed under a given condition. It is required that all the elements of a homogeneous set belong to exactly one of the types T, F, UO, L, HS. All user-defined homogeneous sets are members (instances) of system-defined type HS. It is also possible to define type objects which are subtypes of HS. Homogeneous set is a useful construct needed in design applications. For instance, a homogeneous set of functions defined on a type can thus be used to model its behavior. A defined hierarchy of subtypes of HS can be used to impose a set of constraints on functions or types.

<u>Definition 2.5.</u> A homogeneous set s is a finite set of objects, where $s \in HS$ and is given by

$$s = \{ o_1, o_2, \ldots, o_n \},$$

where $\forall\ o_i \in s,\ \exists\ P \in \{\ T, HS, F, UO, L\ \}\ |\ P(o_i).$

In addition to the type graph of the system-defined objects, the supertype/subtype relations among user-defined objects are represented by a rooted, labeled, acyclic, directed graph, which captures generalization. An instance of any type is also an instance of all its supertypes, and thus inherits a subset——not necessarily proper set——of the operations, functions and rules of its supertypes.

Definition 2.6. *Generalization* is represented as a rooted, labeled, directed, acyclic graph $GG = (V, E)$, where V is a set of vertices, $V \subseteq T_U$ and E is a set of labeled, directed edges,

$$E \subseteq \{ (t_i, t_j, s) \mid t_i, t_j \in V \wedge s \in dom(HS) \wedge \forall f \in s \; t_i \in Arg(f) \}$$

We assume that trivial cycles are present in the generalization graph; that is, $\forall v \in V, \; (v, v, s) \in E$

Arg is a system-defined function which maps members of user-defined function type F_U into the types of their arguments. An edge is defined as a triplet (a, b, s), where a and b are the tail and head of the directed edge such that $b \prec a$, and c is the label of the edge. The root of GG is the system-defined type I_U.

Definition 2.7. The *extended domain* of type $t \in T$ is defined as the union of the extended domains of all t' such that $(t', t, s) \in E$ of GG.

Definition 2.8. The function inheritance by a type t is defined as

$$\forall f \in \bigcup_i s_i \wedge \forall (t_i, t, s_i) \in E \Rightarrow t \in Arg(f)$$

It should be noted that an unlabeled edge $(a, b,)$ implies that it includes all functions, f such that $a \in Arg(f)$. The labeled generalization graph provides a mechanism that specifies full as well as partial function (attribute) inheritance.

Definition 2.9. AT (*AssignedType*) is a mapping from I_U to T_U's power set. It returns one or more types $t \in dom(T_U)$ that are explicitly assigned to an instance object $i \in dom(UO)$.

$$AT : UO \rightarrow 2^{T_U} - \varnothing$$
$$\forall i \in UO \; \exists t \in T_U \mid t \in AT(i) \wedge \neg \exists (t, p, s) \in E \wedge p(i)$$

A notion of *value acquisition* is needed in design databases. This is closely related to the idea of function (attribute) inheritance. The difference is that value acquisition is defined for object instances rather than types. The instance that acquires values will be called *receptor* and the instances from which values are acquired will be called *transmitter*. The type of a receptor either is of the same assigned-type as that of its transmitter or is its subtype. Value acquisition means that a given set of functions returns the same result values for a receptor as for its transmitter. A receptor is not allowed to update the result values of these functions. As in case of attribute inheritance, this notion is further refined by allowing partial value acquisition. Value acquisition is represented by the *instance graph* (*IG*). There exists a mapping from *IG* to $GG = (V, E)$.

$\quad$ <u>Definition 2.10.</u> $\quad IG = (V_I, E_I)$ is a labeled, directed, acyclic graph, where

1. $V_I \subseteq UO$ and $\forall\, i \in V_I \quad \exists\, v \in V \,\land\, v(i)$

2. For each edge $(a, b, s) \in E_I$, $\exists$ a corresponding edge $(x, y, z) \in E$: $x \in AT(a) \,\land\, y \in AT(b) \,\land\, s \in HS \,\land\, s \subseteq z$

3. In *IG*, for each $j \in V_I$, $\exists$ at most one $(i, j, s) \in E_I$ for a corresponding edge $(x, y, z) \in E$ such that $x \in AT(i)$ and $y \in AT(j)$.

4. An edge $(a, b, c) \in E_I \;\Rightarrow\; \forall\, f \in s, \quad f(b) := f(a)$

$\quad$ That is, for every member i in vertex set *Vp* of IG, there exist some type v that is a member of V and i is an instance of v. For every edge in IG, there is a corresponding edge in GG, such that the head and tail in the edge in IG are instances of the corresponding head and tail in the GG edge and the functions that participate in the value acquisition through this edge in IG is a subset of functions inherited through the corresponding edge in IG. For each corresponding edge in GG, there is at most one edge in IG. And lastly, the values of functions returned by the instance object belonging to the head is the same as that of the instance object belonging to the tail of the edge.

Design databases require a facility for defining and manipulating a hierarchically structured set of objects as a single logical entity. We shall call such an entity a *composite* type object, which is defined as a directed acyclic graph where the nodes with in-degree zero are the types of the highest level composite objects, the nodes with out-degree zero are the types of primitive objects. The directed edges in the graph represent the *is-part-of/is-composed-of* relationship between a composite object and its constituents. We shall call this graph the *composition graph (CG)*. At the instance level, the CG is mapped into as many spanning trees, as there are vertices with in-degree zero. The instances of composite object are required to be a strict hierarchy, because of the physical constraint that disallows an object to be a constituent of two distinct composite objects. Sometime an integrity feature is added to CG through the notion of existential dependence, which implies that a constituent object is existentially dependent on its immediate higher level object. We do not support this notion of existential dependence, as it enforces a top-down design strategy. CG provides a means for supporting the notion of composition. A detailed discussion of composite objects, since they are an essential aspect of CAD applications, is provided in Chapter 3.

It should be noted that the notions of aggregation or association are inadequate for modeling this property of composite objects. Composition is an integral property of design objects. This property is deemed indispensable, as it is required for materializing physical objects. Therefore, many constraints are imposed on it; first, its minimum cardinality is always one, which disallows null values in the constituent information of a design object; second, the maximum cardinality, which is not allowed to vary, determines the exact number of constituent objects; third, self-reference is disallowed in this attribute, as it violates the meaningful relationship between a constituent and its composite object. Also, information is maintained to answer queries related to transitive closure of composition.

Definition 2.11. A composition graph (CG) is a directed, acyclic graph, $CG = (V_c, E_c)$, where $V_c \subseteq T_U$ and E_c is a set of directed edges (called *is-composed-of*), where $E_c \subseteq \{(t_i, t_j) \mid t_i, t_j \in V_c\}$. An ordered pair $(x, y) \in E_c$ denotes a directed edge from x to y, which implies that objects of type x are composed of one or more objects of type y.

Definition 2.12. $ICG = (V_d, E_d)$, the instantiated CG, is a directed, acyclic graph, where $V_d \subseteq I_U$ and E_d is a set of directed edges such that $E_d \subseteq \{(i, j) \mid i, j \in V_d\}$. There exists a mapping from ICG to CG.

1. For each $(i, j) \in E_d$, $\exists$ a corresponding edge $(t_i, t_j) \in V_c : t_i(i) \wedge t_j(j)$

2. For each $j \in V_d$, $\exists$ at most one $(i, j) \in E_d$

3. An $i \in V_d$ is said to be *incomplete*, if $\exists$ $(t_i, t_j) \in V_c \wedge t_i(i) \wedge$
    $\neg \exists \ (i, j) \in E_d$

4. For an edge $(a, b) \in E_d$, if b is incomplete, then it implies that a is incomplete.

That is, for every edge in ICG, there is a corresponding edge in CG such that the types of the head and tail of the edge in ICG correspond to the head and tail in the CG edge. The in-degree of of every vertex in ICG is at most one. A vertex in ICG is said to undefined, if it does not have the same out-degree as its corresponding vertex in CG.

2.2 An Example Database

In this section, we shall give a simple example of a database, which will help to explain some of the concepts presented in the previous section. We take an example from a familiar domain without any loss of generality. An example relevant to CAD databases is given in Chapter 3.

This database contains four user-defined types: *person, course, student* and *faculty*. The type *person* has *student* and *faculty* as its subtypes. The type *person* has p1 as an instance; *student* has s1, s2, s3 as instances; *course* has c1, c2, c3 as instances; and faculty has f1, f2 as instances. The following functions are defined on them.

Name (*person*) $\rightarrow$ *charstring u*;

Age (*person*) $\rightarrow$ *integer*;

CName (*course*) $\rightarrow$ *charstring u*;

GPA (*student*) $\rightarrow$ *real*;

Enrollment (*course*) $\rightarrow$ *student* m;

Teaches (*faculty*) $\rightarrow$ *course* m;

The symbols "u" and "m" associated with the result of the above functions represent the unique and multivalued result values, respectively.

A possible scenario for creating the database will be the following. The user will first define some types and specify the subtype/supertype relationships among them; that is, create a generalization graph. After this, functions can be defined on these types. The database can now be populated. Homogeneous sets can be defined at any time provided their elements have already been defined. It is also possible to dynamically add types and functions.

The generalization graph for this database with *UO* as its root is shown along with the proposed system type graph in Figure 2-1. It should be noted that for each database, a different user-defined *GG* will appear under *UO*. The rest of the graph is the system type graph, which is always available. In Figure 2-1, *HS* does not have any subtypes, as we do not make any distinction between user- and system-defined sets at this point. However, the user can define subtypes of *HS*.

The domain of each type is formed by the instances directly assigned to that type. Domains for the types are shown in Figure 2-1. The declarations of domains are self-explanatory. However, explanation is needed for the types F_S and *HS*. It should be recalled that each system-defined type *name* also serves as a predicate function; the functions dom and AT have already been defined. For *HS*, it is assumed that the user has defined two sets {Enrollment, Teaches} and {p1, s2}.

dom (*person*) = { p1 };   dom (*student*) = { s1, s2, s3 };

dom (*course*) = { c1, c2, c3 };   dom (*faculty*) = {f1, f2 };

dom (T_U) = { *person, course, faculty, student* };

dom (T_S) = { U, L, T, HS, F, UO, T_U, T_S, F_U, F_S,

real, integer, Boolean, charstring };

dom (F_U) = { Name, CName, Age, GPA, Enrollment, Teaches };

dom (F_S) = { U, UO, T, HS, F, L, T_U, T_S, F_U, F_S, dom, AT };

dom (*HS*) = { {Enrollment, Teaches}, {p1, s2} };

2.3 Retrieval Using Functions

In this section, we shall present a brief outline of the data manipulation language. For the sake of brevity, syntax for simple declarations of types, subtypes/supertype and instances are omitted here. Some examples in the later sections will illustrate their syntax.

A function is defined by using the following syntax.

Function F-name $(t_1, t_2, \ldots, t_i) \longrightarrow\ < t_{i+1}, \ldots, t_m >$

F-name is an identifier that stands for function name. $t_1, t_2, \ldots, t_i, t_{i+1} \ldots t_m \in T$, are user-defined types, and are not necessarily distinct. The symbols "<" and ">" can be dropped from the declaration, if n is 1 in an n-place tuple. For example, a function called *Age* can be defined in the follwing way.

$$\text{Function Age (Person)} \rightarrow \text{Integer}$$

The update of this function can be performed in the following way.

$$\text{Age (p1)} := 32$$

This data manipulation language is based on domain calculus. Interface variables can be used in queries and updates as references to objects in the result or argument of a function. As in domain calculus, these variables range over the domains of the types they reference. When an object is retrieved into a variable, it is bound to the identifier of the variable which may thereafter be used to refer directly to the object. It is also possible to universally or existentially quantify a variable. A variable referring to a type of the parameters of a function can be omitted, if it is not needed in the formulation of a query.

A query can be expressed by using the following syntax: A | B / P. A contains a list of variables or function names that are being retrieved. B contains the quantification and declaration of the types of variables used in A or P. P is an optional predicate expression that can involve both functions and variables. A function can be derived from one or more defined functions.

This overview describes the logical primitives and the constructs that are essential to illustrate and formalize concepts for design databases. In later sections, some additional features that are needed for dealing with composite objects and versioning will be defined in terms of the basic set of constructs discussed here.

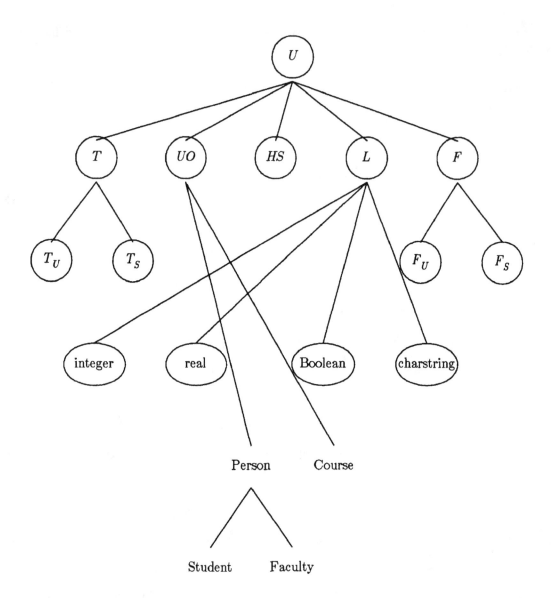

Figure 2-1 The System Type Graph

CHAPTER 3
AN ABSTRACT VIEW OF COMPOSITE OBJECTS

In this section, basic modeling concepts for composite objects are developed. These notions are of fundamental importance for understanding the nature of design objects and their version management.

A composite object, as represented by the composition graph described in Chapter 2, is a recursively defined aggregation of its constituent objects. In the existing literature, the composition property is deemed sufficient to represent a composite object. It is one of the premises of this work that composition, though essential, is inadequate for modeling objects in a complex engineering design.

Objects modeled in engineering applications are assemblies as well as aggregations of their constituent objects that may, in turn, contain other objects. The familiar abstractions of white-box and black-box properties can provide some insight into the nature of design objects. The properties that describe an object without any concern for their internal structure are viewed as black-box properties. The properties that describe the entire structure are looked upon as white-box properties. In the following, we propose a classification of the properties of design objects based on the above abstraction.

External features (EF) of a design object are its non-structural attributes that are visible to the external world.

Internal assembly (IA) of a composite design object is its structural attributes that identify its constituent objects and describe their interrelationships.

24

A *primitive* object does not have any internal assembly properties. It possesses only the external features. In the composition graph, they form the vertices that have out-degree zero.

Thus, external features correspond to black-box properties, as the internal details are not seen, whereas both internal assembly and external features correspond to white-box properties, since entire object is visible. The categorization of the attributes of a composite object into its external features and internal assembly is a useful one. In design applications, it is often desirable to view a composite object as a "primitive" object by disregarding its internal assembly. Also, this classification provides a paradigm for understanding the concept of versioning as it relates to composite objects.

3.1 External Features and Internal Assembly

In this section, we define the different subclasses of attributes mentioned previously. These definitions are by no means formal. However, they provide a framework for understanding the nature of and the requirements for design databases. Later in Section 3.2, an example is given that illustrates these concepts.

The external features can be subdivided into *descriptive* (D_S) and *interface* (I_F) attributes, whereas the internal assembly can be subdivided into *composite aggregation* (C_A), *interconnection* (I_C), and *correspondence* (C_R) attributes.

Interface (I_F) properties describe an abstraction of a design object. These properties define links through which it interacts with the external world; i.e., the user and other design objects. The interface properties are crucial in understanding the nature and functionality of a design object, as they are visible to the external world and present a higher level of abstraction of the internal assembly.

Descriptive (D_S) attributes provide identification and non-interface descriptions of a design object. Properties such as *Name, Designer* etc. are categorized as descriptive attributes.

Composite aggregation (C_A) of a design object identify its immediate constituent objects. This property is captured by the instance composition graph defined in Section 2.1.

Interconnection (I_C) attributes of a composite object represent the interconnections among its constituent objects. These interconnection attributes involve only the interface attributes of the constituent objects.

Correspondence (C_R) attributes of a composite object represent the connection between its interface and the interfaces of its constituent objects.

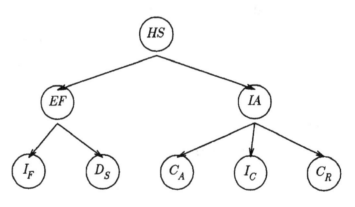

Figure 3-1

We believe that the abstraction of composite objects presented here is independent of any data model. Other models with the construct of homogeneous set can be used. Definition 2.5 introduced the system-defined type *HS* and the notion of homogeneous set. Other system-defined subclasses appear as subtypes of *HS*. The sets of functions defined here will have the following type structure. $EF, IA \prec C$. $I_F, D_S \prec EF$. $C_A, I_C, C_R \prec IA$. This implies that new system-defined set, *EF* and *IA*, become the subtypes of *HS*. The sets, I_F and D_S, are subtypes of *EF*, and they represent the set of attributes that constitute external features. This can be diagrammatically represented in Figure 3-1.

Given these system-defined classes, the functions defined on the type of a design object can be declared as their members. This allows us to enforce any constraint on a class of functions. An example given in the next section will serve to illustrate this point.

3.2 An Example of a Composite Object

Consider a circuit representation of a 4-bit adder. Figure 3-2 shows its interface specification: a pair of 4-bit numbers (X, Y) are inputs, a 5-bit number representing their sum (Z) is output. It can have other descriptive attributes, *Name, Designer*, etc., which are not shown in the figure. The internal assembly of this adder is shown in Figure 3-3. It contains four adder-slices. The interface of adder-slice is given in Figure 3-4. The interface properties of adder-slice are inputs X, Y (1-bit numbers) and C_{in} (the carry from a previous slice) and outputs C_{out} (carry) and Z (1-bit sum).

The internal assembly of the adder-slice is diagrammatically shown in Figure 3-5. The composite aggregation of this adder-slice is given by three constituent objects: half-adder1, half-adder2 and OR-gate. Half-adder1 and half-adder2 themselves are composite objects. For the purposes of this example, we assume that OR-gate is a primitive object, and thus has no internal assembly. Interconnections are shown between the output of half-adder1 and the input of half-adder2, between the output of half-adder1 and the input of OR-gate, etc. Correspondences are shown between input X of adder-slice and an input of half-adder1, between output C_{out} of adder-slice and an output of OR-gate, etc. As mentioned in the previous section, the interconnection and correspondence functions are defined only in terms of the interface properties. Also, as shown in Figures 3-3 and 3-5, only the external features (which include the interface properties) of a constituent object are visible to its composite object or to the external world.

Figures 3-7 and 3-8 show the interface and the internal assembly of half-adder. Half-adder contains an AND-gate and an XOR-gate, which are again assumed to be primitive objects. The internal assembly of Figure 3-7 does not have any interconnection attributes.

Adder forms the root of composition aggregation hierarchy, which has three levels. The first level contains adder-slices. The second level has half-adders and OR-gate. The leaves of the hierarchy are given by AND-gates and XOR-gates. Figure 3-6 shows an alternative design of the internal assembly of adder-slice; in this design, the aggregation hierarchy of adder has only two levels.

3.3 Modeling Composite Objects

In this section, we present intensional and extensional descriptions of adder-slice using the constructs defined in Chapter 2. An identifier that starts with a lower case letter denotes a type and an identifier that starts with an upper case letter are instances of some type. This convention has been adopted here just for convenience and comprehensibility. We allow any legal identifier. In the function definitions, two key letters, "u" and "m", are used to signify that the function returns unique- or multi-valued results.

We assume that the following types have been declared: *adderslice, halfadder, orgate, xorgate, andgate* and *terminal.* All but *terminal* are design objects. The following functions are defined on these type to model the composite object, addersilce.

function TName (*terminal*) → *charstring* u

function IOtype (*terminal*) → *char*

function ORName (*orgate*) → *charstring* u

function ORInput (*orgate*) → *terminal* m

function OROutput (*orgate*) → *terminal* u

function HName (*halfadder*) → *charstring* u

function HInput (*halfadder*) → *terminal* m

function HOutput (*halfadder*) → *terminal* m

function HContains (*halfadder*) → <*xorgate, andgate*>

function HLink1 (*halfadder, terminal*) → <*xorgate, terminal*> m

function HLink2 (*halfadder, terminal*) → <*andgate, terminal*> m

Functions HName, HInput and HOutput constitute the external features of object type *halfadder*, whereas functions HInput and HOutput define the interface. Functions HContains, HLink1 and HLink2 define the internal assembly. This internal assembly does not have any interconnection attributes. HContains defines the composition aggregation and the other two functions define the correspondence.

function AName (*adderslice*) → *charstring* u

function ADesigner (*adderslice*) → *charstring*

function AInput (*adderslice*) → *terminal* u, m

function AOutput (*adderslice*) → *terminal* u, m

function AContains (*adderslice*) → <*halfadder, halfadder, orgate*>

function AConnect1 (*adderslice, halfadder, halfadder*) → <*terminal, termi-nal*>

function AConnect2 (*adderslice, halfadder, orgate*) → <*terminal, terminal*>

function ALink1 (*adderslice, terminal*) $\rightarrow$ $<$*halfadder, terminal*$>$

function ALink2 (*adderslice, terminal*) $\rightarrow$ $<$*orgate, terminal*$>$

AContains defines the composite aggregation of *adderslice*. Functions AConnect1 and AConnect2 describe the interconnection among the constituents of adder-slice. AConnect1 provides a mapping from the composite object, adder-slice, and its constituents, two half-adders to a pair of terminals through which the interfaces of these half-adders are connected. Similarly, AConnect2 provides a mapping from the composite object, adder-slice, and its constituents, a half-adder and an OR-gate, to a pair of terminals through which the interfaces of half-adder and ORgate are connected. Functions ALink1 and ALink2 define the correspondence properties. Alink1 describes a mapping from adder-slice and one of its interface (defined in terms of a terminal) to the constituent object half-adder and its interface. Similarly, ALink2 describes a mapping from adder-slice and one of its interface attribute to its component OR-gate and its interface. The other functions are self-explanatory.

In Section 3.1, we described some system-defined classes. For each design type object, a subset of the functions defined on them can be declared as a member of one the subclasses. For instance, we have, for *adderslice*, the following relationships.

$\{$ AName, ADesigner $\}$ $\in$ D_S

$\{$ AInput, AOutput $\}$ $\in$ I_F

$\{$ AContains $\}$ $\in$ C_A

$\{$ AConnect1, AConnect2 $\}$ $\in$ I_C

$\{$ ALink1, ALink2 $\}$ $\in$ C_R

We present a partial extension of adder-slice. We assume the types declared above have been instantiated and thus we have the following domains.

$$\text{dom}(\textit{terminal}) = \{ \text{X, Y, Z, CI, CO, A1, B1, A2, B2, S1, S2, C1, C2, I1, I2, J} \}$$

$$\text{dom}(\textit{orgate}) = \{ \text{OR-gate} \}$$

$$\text{dom}(\textit{halfadder}) = \{ \text{HalfAdder1, HalfAdder2} \}$$

$$\text{dom}(\textit{adderslice}) = \{ \text{AdderSlice1} \}$$

The assignment of values to the functions for OR-gate and for *some* of the instances of terminal are shown here.

TName (X) := "X" ;   IOType (X) := "I";

TName (Z) := "Z" ;   IOType (Z) := "O";

ORName (OR-gate) := "OR-Gate";

ORInput (OR-gate) := $\{$ I1, I2 $\}$;

OROutput (OR-gate) := J ;

HName (HalfAdder1) := "Half-Adder1";

HInput (HalfAdder1) := $\{$ A1, B1 $\}$;

HOutput (HalfAdder1) := $\{$ S1, C1 $\}$;

HName (HalfAdder2) := "Half-Adder2";

HInput (HalfAdder2) := $\{$ A2, B2 $\}$;

HOutput (HalfAdder2) := $\{$ S2, C2 $\}$;

AName (AdderSlice1) := "Adder-Slice1";

Designer (AdderSlice1) := "Ostrominsky";

AInput (AdderSlice1) := $\{$ X, Y, CI $\}$;

AOutput (AdderSlice1) := $\{$ Z, CO $\}$;

AContains (AdderSlice1) := $<$ HalfAdder1, HalfAdder2, OR-gate $>$;

AConnect1 (AdderSlice1, HalfAdder1, HalfAdder2) := $<$ S1, B2 $>$;

AConnect2 (AdderSlice1, HalfAdder1, OR-gate) := < C1, I1 >;

AConnect2 (AdderSlice1, HalfAdder2, OR-gate) := < C2, I2 >;

ALink1 (AdderSlice1, X) := < HalfAdder1, A1 >;

ALink1 (AdderSlice1, Y) := < HalfAdder1, B1 >;

ALink1 (AdderSlice1, CI) := < HalfAdder2, A2 >;

ALink1 (AdderSlice1, Z) := < HalfAdder2, S2 >;

ALink2 (AdderSlice1, CO) := < OR-gate, J >;

The above example shows the modeling capabilities of the proposed constructs. The functional paradigm of this data model can represent complex design features. It should also be noted that even simple design objects, as illustrated by the example, cannot be represented at the type level alone. The design objects and their functions have to be instantiated in order to unambiguously specify the interconnection, aggregation and correspondence properties. As we shall see in the next chapter, this observation has important implications to the concepts employed in version management.

3.4 Rules for Building Composite Objects

There are essentially two ways to build a composite design object. First, a design object is defined initially in terms of its external features and later its internal assembly is described and instantiated. Second, a composite object, viewed as an abstraction of a set of components into a higher level object, are built from its already defined and instantiated constituent objects. These two approaches lead to the top-down and bottom-up design strategies. We disallow neither of these strategies nor any of their combination, and thus provides a flexible system where designers have the freedom to pursue any design strategy. In the following, some integrity rules for building composite objects are given. A reference to *constituent object* will imply that there exists a composite type object whose composite aggregation includes the type of that object. If there does not exist such a composite type object, the object will be referred to as a *non-constituent* object. Such a distinction is necessary, since objects can be defined at any stage of the design. Hence, a non-constituent object can evolve into a constituent object and a primitive object can change into a composite object.

Rule 3.1. A constituent object can be contained (referenced) by at most one composite object (Definition 2.12.2).

Rule 3.2. A composite object is said to be incomplete, if the references to any of its constituents are not bound (Definition 2.12.3). That is, their constituents are declared at the type level, but not completely instantiated.

Rule 3.3. A composite object is said to be incomplete, if one or more of its constituents are incomplete. (Definition 3.12.4)

Rule 3.4. A modification in the interface properties of a composite object may necessitate modifications in the interface properties of its components. (This downward propagation of modifications may not always be necessary, if it is accompanied with the modifications in the correspondence and interconnection attributes of the composite object.)

Rule 3.5. A modification in the internal assembly, C_A, I_C, or C_R, of a composite object object does not have any effect on its constituent objects.

Rule 3.6. A constituent object is *not* considered existentially dependent on its composite object. Thus, deletion of a composite object does not result in the deletion of its constituents, only the composite object itself and the functions defined on it are deleted. A cascaded deletion must be specified as such.

These rules appear to be adequate for defining the innate characterisics of design objects. However, these rules have been formulated without taking into account the dimension of versioning. In Chapter 4, we shall present a framework for version management. We shall also examine whether these rules need to be extended or relaxed in the context of versioned design objects.

It should be noted that the subdivision of *EF* and *IA* discussed in this chapter may not always be adequate. Further experience in structural/mechanical engineering design is needed to test the above subdivision and verify its adequacy.

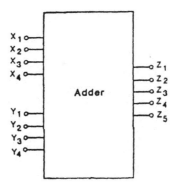

Figure 3-2

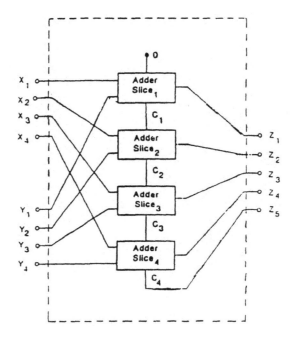

Figure 3-3

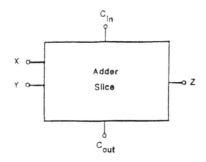

Figure 3-4

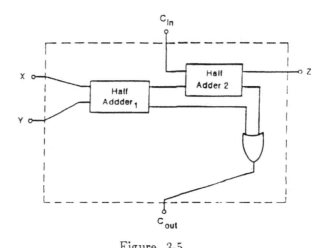

Figure 3-5

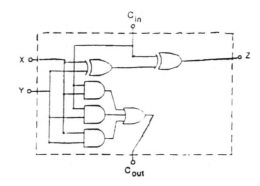

Figure 3-6

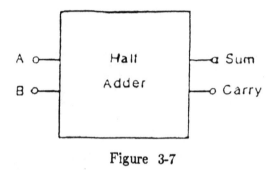

Figure 3-7

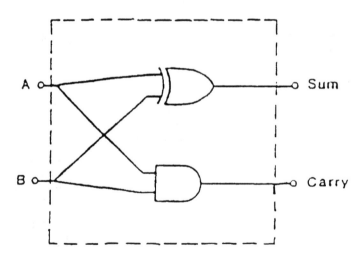

Figure 3-8

CHAPTER 4
VERSION CONTROL AND MANAGEMENT

Generally, design of an object starts with a high level description of some aspects of that object. A named collection of information describing an object at the type level is called a *template*, which can be modeled by a type and a set of functions defined on it.

A design object is something that retains an identity throughout the period in which it evolves through the design process that may change its state. *Versions* are snapshots of the object in different states and are modeled by objects that are distinct from each other, though they share some identifiable common characteristics. The versions of a design object contain qualitatively or quantitatively different information, but they evolve in the direction of an ultimate design goal. A version contains sufficient information to instantiate the object. If the version object is composite, then its references are bound to its versioned or non-versioned constituent objects.

There is considerable debate in the literature as to when two instances of the same type are different objects and when they are merely different versions of the same object. The key to deciding this issue is to view different attributes of a design object as either extrinsic or intrinsic attributes. The intrinsic property describe the essence of the object. If intrinsic properties change, so does the object. Extrinsic properties, on the other hand, can be modified without changing the object in any significant way. Interface is an example of intrinsic attributes, whereas properties such as "designer", "co-ordinate position", and even internal assembly are examples of extrinsic attributes. In enginnering design, there are many situations where the same

38

interface can be materialized from different implementations—internal assemblies—of an object. For example, Figure 3.4 and Figure 3.5 show an Adder-Slice, its interface, and its internal assembly respectively. Figure 3.6 presents a different internal assembly for the same object Adder-Slice. This internal assembly contains a different set of constituent objects, but shares the same interface (shown in Fig. 3.4) and provides the same functionality.

One of our basic theses is that different versions of a design object share the same interface but have different internal assemblies. If the interface properties change, this implies that the object itself has changed in some fundamental way. Several arguments can be put forth in the support of this hypothesis.

1. Interface defines the functionality of the object and is visible to the external world.

2. Design objects interact—correspond, interconnect—with one another through interface.

3. A composite object enters into correspondence relationships with the interface properties of its constituents. Therefore, any modification of the interface of an object may disqualify it from being used as a component of its composite object.

4. Changes in the internal assembly of an object, if its interface remains invariant, are not visible to the external world and may thus warrant creation of only a different version.

Therefore, we maintain that different versions of an object share the same interface properties and some descriptive attributes but can differ from one another in their internal structure both at the type and instance levels.

4.1 Generic, Versioned and Unversioned Objects

In this section, we discuss three system-defined types, which provide the basic framework for our proposed methodologies for version management.

Each design object, in addition to possessing its own types, belongs to one of three system-defined types: *Versioned*, *Generic*, or *Unversioned*, which are subtypes of *DesignObject*. Generic objects are instance of type *Generic*. The instances of type *Versioned* are versioned objects, which are also called versions. Design objects which are not going through a process of evolution are instances of type *Unversioned*. These three types are mutually exclusive. It should also be possible to dynamically acquire and discard one of these types. The protocol of such conversion is discussed in Section 4.2.2. We stipulate that only design objects are versionable.

The common characteristics that are used to relate all versions of a design object are called its *invariant* properties. Invariance, however, does not imply that they can never be modified; it means that they are invariant over the version set.

A *generic* design object is characterized by its invariant external features, which subsumes the interface properties. Therefore, a generic object identifies the design object, represents its essence and contains a high level abstraction of its functionality.

In this model, all versions of a design object, which are allowed to have different types, value-acquire (Definition 2.10) the invariant external features from its generic object. The type of a versioned object appears in the generalization graph as a subtype of the generic object type, if they are of different assigned-types. Furthermore, the versioned objects appear as receptors with the generic object as their transmitter in the instance graph. There is only one generic object for each version set. This scheme provides a paradigm that relates all versions of a design object and also ensures that they have identical interface attributes.

A number of functions can be defined to relate a generic object and its versions and to model their basic properties. Some of these system-defined functions are shown here.

GenericInst (Versioned) $\longrightarrow$ Generic;

FirstVersion (Generic) $\longrightarrow$ Versioned;

InitialVersions (Generic) $\longrightarrow$ Versioned m;

VersionSet (Generic) $\longrightarrow$ Versioned m;

ImmedSuccessor (Versioned) $\longrightarrow$ Versioned ;

ImmedPredecessor (Versioned) $\longrightarrow$ Versioned ;

VersionNumber (Versioned) $\longrightarrow$ Integer;

CreationTime (Versioned) $\longrightarrow$ TimeStamp;

VersionStatus (Versioned) $\longrightarrow$ Status.

GenericInst maps a versioned object onto its generic object, from which it acquires its invariant attributes. *FirstVersion* returns the earliest version of the version set. *InitialVersion* returns the set of all the versions which are initially created and have no predecessors. These versions are considered alternatives (to be explained later) of the design. *VersionNumber* returns the version identifier that is unique within a version set. Other functions are self-explanatory.

4.1.1 Version Graph

A version graph captures the evolution history of versioned objects. We define a *version graph (VG)* as a disconnected, acyclic, directed graph. The edges of this graph represent the successor/predecessor relationship. The version graph $VG = (V_v, E_v)$, where $V_v \subseteq$ *Versioned* and E_v is a set of directed edges :

1. $\forall v, w \in V_v,$ GenericInst (v) = GenericInst (w).

2. $\exists$ a partition, $\{(V_1, E_1), (V_2, E_2),..(V_i, E_i),..(V_n, E_n)\}$ of VG, where each member of this partition is a connected subgraph.

3. For each subgraph (V_i, E_i), $\exists$ exactly one $v \in V_i$ such that $indegree(v) = 0$.

Figure 4-1 shows an example of a version graph. The roots of the subgraphs, D.v1 and D.v6, are the objects returned by function *InitialVersions*. These versions can be viewed as different alternatives of a design. The non-root versions in a subgraph can be looked upon as the refinements of the alternative design that forms the root of a subgraph. For example, D.v5 has been derived from D.v1, and is thus its refinement. Versions in a subgraph are derived from each other and hence have the same user-defined types. As mentioned earlier, the roots of subgraphs are not necessarily of the same type.

All the versions in a version graph, that is V_v, is referred to as a version set. Versions in the version set are considered equivalent, as they have identical invariant attributes. In the forthcoming discussion, we use the term *equivalent* versions for the members of the same version set.

4.1.2 Versioning at the Type and Instance Levels

In the literature, it has often been felt that versioning should be allowed both at the type level and instance level. Versioning at the instance level implies that different versions of the same object differ only in the *values* of some of their properties. Versioning at the type level, on the other hand, means that equivalent version can have different assigned types. It has an added implication that modifications of a template——a type and a collection of attributes defined on it——creates another template version. Furthermore, there is an underlying assumption that a template is adequate for providing a complete description of a design object.

Some schemes, which advocate versioning at the type level, propose that a derived version should be a subtype of its predecessor version, so that a design may evolve through incremental steps, as successor versions inherit all attributes of their predecessors besides having their own properties. This scheme puts an unnatural constraint on the design process by imposing an incremental strategy. Most systems, however, provide versioning at the instance level, since versioning at the type level is not without its problems. First, it is quite a deviation from the traditional notions of data and databases. Second, templates often prove to be insufficient in providing a complete description of a design object, since many attributes still need instantiated values. Third, in many applications, e.g., software design, versioning at the type level has no relevance at all.

The proposed scheme brings about a compromise between the two opposing views. Versioning remains at the instance level in the sense that all information is required to be instantiated. However, versions can have entirely different types and thus different internal assembly properties. These disparate types of various versions are related together by the generic object and the mechanism of value-acquisition of invariant attributes.

For instance, in Figure 4-1, let the generic object, D.g, be of assigned-type X, and the versions, D.v1 and D.v6 be of assigned-types Y and Z respectively; Y and Z are subtypes of X. D.v1 and D.v6 are related by the imposition of invariant attribute acquisition from D.g.

4.2   Creation and Updatability of Versions

To model the dynamic behavior of versions, the system should be able to record significant changes in the evolution history of design. This requires categorizing the functions (attributes) of versioned objects into different classes. It should be emphasized that a design object itself is a complex structure, which has different classes of attributes even in unversioned state.

4.2.1   Classification of Version Attributes

We present a classification of attributes of design objects. The notion of class, defined in Section 2.4, is used to model behavior of a design object on the updatability of various groups of functions.

Figures 4-2, 4-3 and 4-4 show the classification of functions for unversioned, generic, and versioned objects respectively. $D_S{}^1$ and $D_S{}^2$ form a partition of descriptive attributes D_S. Figure 4-3 does not show any internal assembly attributes, since generic objects, by definition, do not possess any internal structure. In Figure 4.4, @ stands for invariant attributes, * represents *version-significant* attributes and # stands for *nonversion-significant* attributes. These terms will be defined shortly. It should be noted that in Figure 4-4 all interface attributes are value-acquired from the generic object instance and $D_S{}^2$ are attributes inherited from the generic object type. It should be recalled that value-acquisition implies attribute inheritance.

The three classes of attributes, invariant, *version-significant* and *nonversion-significant*, provide a mechanism for controlling update propagation in versions.

Version-significant attributes can be updated only in a non-destructive manner. Conceptually, modifications in one of these attributes creates a new derived versioned object bearing the change. Such creations of new version are called mutation. There is an important exception to this rule. The replacement of equivalent versions by one another in the internal assembly functions, though they are defined to be version-significant, does *not* cause mutation. This rule provides a mechanism for effectively controlling unnecessary proliferation of versions. In the forthcoming discussion, we refer to this update as *equivalence modification*.

Nonversion-significant attributes of an object can always be modified without causing any mutation.

The invariant attributes of versioned object cannot be modified at the version level, since they are value-acquired from the generic object.

The three classes invariant, version-significant and nonversion-significant can be defined as subtypes of C, and different functions can be accordingly declared as their members.

4.2.2 Version States and Operations

A feature that provides "automatic" generation of a new version on the modification of version-significant attributes would be quite convenient. However, in design applications, modifications are rarely atomic; normally, they are batched updates. For instance, if the component aggregation properties are modified, this can require modifications in interconnection and correspondence attributes.

In order to provide nonatomic updates and to maintain the constraints of version-significant and nonversion-significant properties, we stipulate that a versioned object be in either of the following three states: *validated*, *stable* and *transient*. The characteristics of these three version states are described below

Validated versions have the following characteristics:

1. No modification is allowed on validated versions.

2. All the constituent references in a validated version must be bound either to unversioned or other validated versions.

3.   Concurrent access is allowed on them.

4.   New versions can be derived from them.

Stable versions have the following characteristics:

1.   Their version-significant attributes cannot be modified subject to the exception of equivalence modification.

2.   Nonversion-significant attributes can be modified.

3.   New versions can be derived from stable versions.

4.   Concurrent access is provided on them.

Transient versions have the following characteristics:

1.   All noninvariant attributes of a transient versions can be modified.

2.   All newly created and derived versions begin in the transient state.

3.   New versions cannot be derived from them.

The following table summarizes the updatability of versions in the three states.

	Invariant	Version siginificant	Nonversion significant
Transient	No	Yes	Yes
Stable	No	No *	Yes
Validated	No	No	No

* Subject to the exception of equivalence modification

Table 4-1

Since in this model automatic generation of versions are disallowed, modifications in the version significant attributes of an object can be achieved by deriving a new version, which is a copy of the given version object, in transient state and performing the modifications on this version. Four operations and their detailed protocols are discussed below.

Promote is an operation defined on transient or stable versioned objects. When applied to transient or stable versions, it changes their states to stable or validated statuses respectively.

Create is an operation defined on a generic object for creating a new transient versioned object from the generic object. It entails the following steps:

1. This operation requires a mandatory specification of a user-defined type along with the identifier of the generic object.

2. An object of the given type as well as of type *Versioned* is created, and it is assigned a version number.

3. It is made to value-acquire the invariant attributes from the generic object. No values are assigned to its other attributes.

4. It is inserted as a root in the version graph. This version is returned by function InitialVersions.

5. This versioned object starts in the transient state. The promote operation, which may follow possible modifications, changes this version to the stable state.

Derive is an operation defined on stable or validated versioned objects. It creates a copy of the operand version in the transient state, and assigns it a version number. It entails the following steps:

1. A new object of the same types as the given versioned object is created and a version number is assigned to it.

2. It is made to value-acquire all the invariant attributes from the generic object of the given version. All other attribute values, with the exception of the functions defined on type *Versioned*, are copied from the given version.

3. It is inserted in the version graph as an immediate successor of the given version.

4. The derived version starts in the transient state.

5. The promote operation, which may follow possible modifications, changes its state to the stable status.

   Convert is an operation that converts an existing unversioned object into a generic object with its first version. It entails the following steps:

1. The type generic is added to this object.

2. A new object of the same user-defined type as well as of type Versioned is created. It is made to value inherit all the invariant attributes from the generic object.

3. All other attribute values of the generic object are copied to this versioned object.

4. It is assigned a version number and is inserted in the version graph as a root of a subgraph. (This version is returned by function FirstVersion.)

5. The internal assembly properties of the generic object, if any, are deleted.

   In Figure 4.5, the transition diagram shows the effect of applying these operations on unversioned, generic and versioned objects. The dashed arrow signifies that the object itself undergo change, whereas the solid arrows means that the object remains unchanged, and that these operations give rise to a new object.

4.2.3 Copying of Versioned Composite Objects

   In the context of creating or deriving a version, references have been made to the operation of copying. In this section, the details of copying is discussed.

   One of the reasons why no consensus could be achieved on several aspects of version management is the fact that the boundary of a design object is not clearly defined. In conventional databases, an object can enter into any number of associations with other objects, and any changes in the object is directly or indirectly propagated to other such objects. This is not true in design databases.

The abstractions we have proposed in this model allow us to delineate the boundaries of a design object. The interface properties are essential in understanding the nature of design objects and its boundaries. Interconnection and correspondence are the only relationships through which a design object interacts with other design objects. Furthermore, these interactions involve the invariant interface. As noted before, we stipulate that only design objects are versionable. Consequently, the boundaries of a design object can be distinctly delineated by its external features and its internal assembly, since they are necessary and sufficient to instantiate the object. This implies that for a constituent object the composite object that references it and other constituent objects that interact with it lie *beyond* its physical and conceptual boundaries.

Copying of a version object is defined as the creation of another versioned object, which is assigned unique object identifier and version number, and which possesses identical external features and internal assembly. Thus, a newly created or derived version is *not* referenced by any composite object. The values of functions defined on type *Versioned* such as CreationTime, VersionNumber, etc. must be different.

In case of composite objects, copying of internal assembly implies that a versioned or unversioned object can appear as a constituent object in more than one composite objects. This seems to violate Rule 4.1, which requires that a design object can be a component of at most one composite object. In Section 4.4, we shall review the rules given in Chapter 3.

4.2.4 Version Proliferation

As versioned objects may themselves contain other versioned objects as constituents, an uncontrolled propagation of update can proliferate to the top. The composite aggregation is defined to be version-significant, and thus its modification must cause mutation. However, the proposed methodology, by viewing all versions in a version set as equivalent and interchangeable, provides the capability for exploring and experimenting with different versions of a constituent object without having to create a new version of its composite object. The designer, however, has the option of creating a new version and incorporating the changes there.

An example should illustrate the point. In Figure 4-6, a versioned object A.v1 has two constituent objects B.v1 and C.v2; B.v1, in turn, contains D.v2 and E.v5 and C.v2 contains F.v3 and G.v6. Suppose a new version D.V5 is derived from D.v2. (Its version graph is shown in Figure 4-1.) B.v1 changes its reference from D.v2 to D.v5, which is shown in Figure 4-7. Since B.v1 has undergone equivalence modification, no new version of B.v1 need to be created. However, it is possible to derive a new version B.v2 (not shown in the figures) from B.v1 and to replace D.v2 by D.v5 in B.v2. Again, either B.v2 can simply replace B.v1 in A.v1's assembly or a new version, A.v2, can be derived from A.v1 and the change can be incorporated in A.v2. Thus, the designer has the option, at every level of composition hierarchy, to choose from one of the two strategies.

Let us consider another scenario. The internal assembly of C.v2 need to be changed by adding a new object H.v1 to its composite aggregation and updating its interconnections and correspondence. (We assume that it has no effect on the interface of C.v2). This cannot be done without mutating C.v2. Thus, a new version C.v3 is derived from C.v2 and necessary modification are made in C.v3, as shown in Figure 4-7. Either C.v2 can be replaced by C.v3 in the internal assembly of A.v1 or A.v1 is mutated. Figure 4-7 represents the situation where a replacement is made in the composition aggregation of A.v1 without causing any mutation.

We can summarize these two options as following. One, the designer can explore different configurations of a composite object by applying equivalence modifications to its internal assembly, which does cause mutation. Two, the designer can derive a new version in a transient state and incorporate those changes there; this option can be used at every level of composition hierarchy. These protocols allow a controlled update propagation and version proliferation.

4.3 Dynamic Binding and Generic Objects

In a design environment, a facility is frequently desired which allows an indirect form of addressing, whereby composite objects can make "generic" references to constituent objects. These references provide dynamic binding, as they may at some later time be coerced to refer to some specific versions of the object under some default criteria. The utility of this scheme is clear. A designer may want to take advantage to the improvements made to an object, and thus by making a generic references to that object, the designer can use the delayed resolution of the reference to choose a default version. The other advantage is that a designer can use a generic reference as a place-holder for some constituent object without any concern for or commitment to its actual implementation. This is particularly useful in situations where several designers are working on different divisions of a design.

When a composite object makes reference to a specific version of its constituent object, it is said to be statically bound to that version; whereas when the reference is generic, the composite object is said to be dynamically bound to some default version of the constituent object. So far, we have discussed only static binding.

In this model, the generic instance object is used for dynamic binding. Every generic object instance has at least one user-defined type and the system-defined type *Generic*. It also possesses the interface attributes, and thus can participate in the interconnection and correspondence properties of a composite object. Furthermore, all functions in the internal assembly of a composite object can be defined in terms of the user-defined types of its generic constituent object. This scheme provides the facility for substituting a generic object by any of its versions, which is either of the same type as the generic object or its subtype.

Therefore, a composite object can reference a generic constituent object in its internal assembly. The generic object conceptually represents the entire version set and can be dereferenced to any version of the set. The version object to which the generic object is deferenced is called a *default* version, and is selected from the version set according to some predefined criteria. For example, the criterion can be to select a version with the latest time-stamp. The system-defined function *Default* is given below.

$$Default \; (Generic) \; \longrightarrow \; Versioned \; \; u$$

The generic object serves a dual purpose. On the one hand, it is used to relate all its version objects; on the other hand, it is used in a generic reference for dynamic binding.

4.4 Rules for Versioned Composite Objects

In view of composite references of versioned objects, we shall furnish new rules that will supplant some of the rules given in Section 3.4. For a precise formulation of these rules, we define a function G for design objects.

$$G\,(x) \; \longrightarrow \; \begin{cases} GenericInst\,(x) & \text{if } Versioned\,(x) \\ x & \text{if } Unversioned\,(x) \; \lor \; Generic\,(x) \end{cases}$$

G maps a design object onto itself, if it is of type *Generic* or *Unversioned*; otherwise, it maps it into its generic object.

Rule 4.1. The single-valuedness of the mapping from a constituent to its composite object is determined by applying function G on these objects.

As Rule 3.1 states, every constituent object instance maps into a single composite object that contains it. Rule 4.1 relaxes this constraint by allowing any constituent object instance, which can be of type *Generic, Versioned*, or *Unversioned*, to be referenced by more than one equivalent versions. By applying function G on different versions of a composite object, we get the same generic object, whereby the mapping remains single-valued. The other related question is whether different versions of a constituent object can be referenced by different composite objects, which may either be unversioned or versioned. Again, application of G on the equivalent versions of a constituent object returns an identical generic object, and the constraint is violated, only if it is being referenced by *different* generic or unversioned composite objects.

The examples given in Figure 4-8 and Figure 4-9 help explain the rule. In Figure 4-8, all the links from composite object to constituent objects are valid, since the mapping to the composite generic instance does not violate the single-valuedness. B.v3 has two composite object links, but the application of G on A.v1 and A.v2 return their generic instance A.g. The case for B.g is similar. In Figure 4-9, on the other hand, any combination of *two* or more crossed-out links violate the constraint. Application of G on D.v3, D.g and D.v4 return D.g, which is referenced by different composite objects.

The rule given above is close to reality, as it treats different versions as equivalent design objects. They are considered different manifestations of the same object with the underlying assumption that in the final phase of design only one of the multitude of versions will be designated as the accepted version.

Rules 3.2 and 3.3 need no modifications. However, it should be noted that either specific or generic binding is deemed sufficient.

Rule 3.4 needs an addendum. In case of versioned objects, the interface properties are considered invariant. Hence, they cannot be modified at the version level. These modifications can be performed only on generic objects.

Rule 4.2. The interface values of a versioned composite objects can be modified only at the generic level.

Rule 3.5, on the other hand, needs to be supplanted by the following rule.

Rule 4.3. A modification in the internal assembly of a version object gives rise to another version except in the case when a constituent is replaced by an equivalent versioned or generic object.

The Rule 3.6 remains valid. However, a rule is required to deal with the deletion of generic objects.

Rule 4.4. All version objects in a set are considered existentially dependent on its generic object. Therefore, deletion of a generic object will result in the deletion of all its versions.

Table 4-2 shows the correspondence, if any, between the rules given in Chapter 3 and the rules needed in the context of versioning.

In this chapter, we discussed basic modeling concepts and protocols for managing and controlling versions of composite objects. A precise definition of versions for design objects was given, version graph was defined, and two states for versioned objects were proposed. A protocol was provided for controlling update propagation and version proliferation. A notion of generic object was introduced in order to relate members of a version set and to provide dynamic binding. A methodology was proposed to deal with versioning at the instance and template levels. A number of rules were also given for providing a consistent semantics of composite version objects.

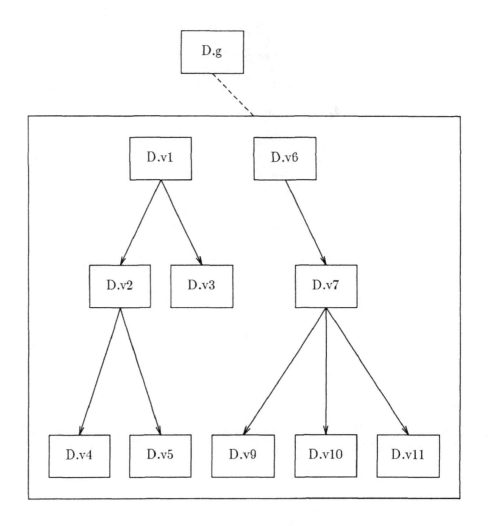

Figure 4-1

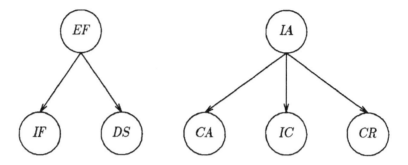

Figure 4-2   Unversioned Object

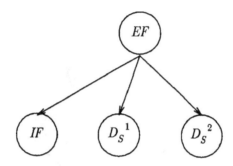

Figure 4-3   Generic Object

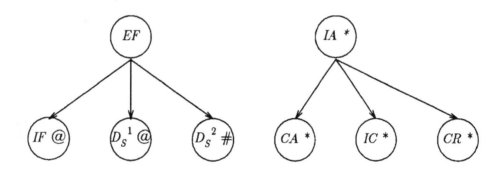

Figure 4-4   Versioned Object

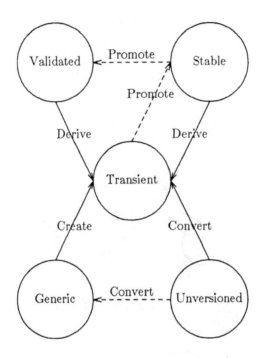

Figure 4-5

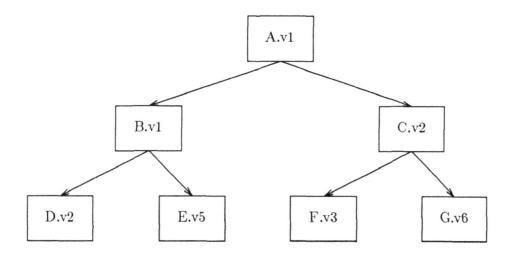

Figure 4-6

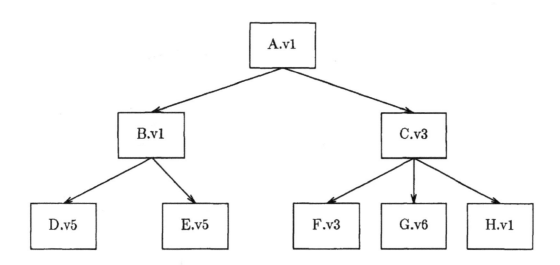

Figure 4-7

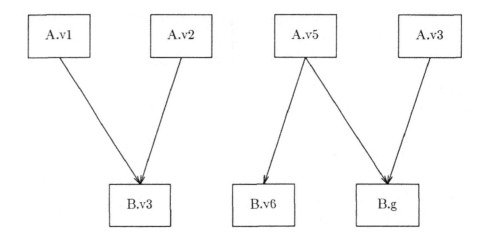

Figure 4-8

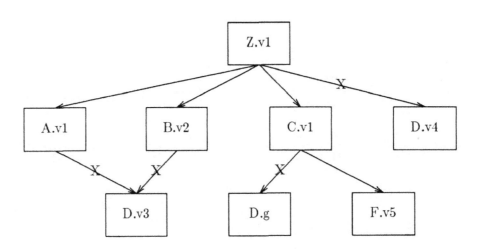

Figure 4-9

Rules for Composite Objects	Rules for Versioned Composite Objects	Remark
Rule 3.1	Rule 4.1	Supplanted
Rule 3.2		Valid
Rule 3.3		Valid
Rule 3.4	Rule 4.2	Addendum
Rule 3.5	Rule 4.3	Supplanted
Rule 3.4	Rule 4.2	Addendum
Rule 3.6		Valid
	Rule 4.4	Addition

Table 4-2

CHAPTER 5
MAINTENANCE OF CONSISTENT SEMANTICS FOR COMPOSITE OBJECTS

The data model that we propose for design applications has several complex constructs such as composition, generalization, version and instance graphs and instance composition graph. These constructs interact with and interdepend upon one another.

We have shown that a mapping exists from the instance graph (Definition 2.10) to the generalization graph (Definition 2.6), and have given some rules for imposing integrity for this mapping. Similarly, it was shown (Definition 2.12) that a mapping from the instance composition graph (ICG) to the composition graph (Definition 2.11) exists; the related rules of this mapping were also given.

In this chapter, we study the interdependence among these constructs in order to provide rules for enforcing consistent semantics and algorithms. These are necessary for handling different problems associated with the effects of their updates upon one another.

5.1 Protocols for Insertions and Deletions

In this section, some constraints that are essential for imposing consistency in design databases are outlined.

Any addition of a new node in GG with no immediate predecessor is made an immediate successor to the virtual node I_u (Figure 2-1). This is necessary, since GG is, by definition, a rooted graph.

61

In the forthcoming discussion, we use the convention established in Chapter 2 whereby a directed edge is represented as an ordered binary relation (x, y), which means that there is a path from x to y. For GG, an edge (x, y) implies that y is a subtype of x; for CG it means that y is a constituent of x.

Addition of a new edge (A, B) in GG results in B inheriting all functions of A and its predecessors. (A, B) must not create a cycle. Additions and deletions in the functions defined on a node in GG are propagated to all its successors. Removal of an edge (A, B) from GG results in B's loosing all functions inherited from A and its predecessors. If A is the only predecessor of B, then B is made an immediate successor of the virtual root I_u. This explains the mechanism of attribute inheritance in GG.

Removal of a node A in GG is possible only if there does not exist an instance object x such that $AT(x) = A$. The Definition 2.9 explains AT. Removal of a node thus results in the removal of all edges directed to its immediate successors and all edges directed to it from its immediate predecessors. This implies that a type cannot be deleted as long as one or more of its instances exist. Also, the successor/predecessor relationship is considered fundamental; that is, its deletion implies the loss of all transitive relations.

Addition of an edge (A, B) in CG results in checking GG for a cascaded update of CG. This implies that attribute inheritance also applies to composition. Thus, if a node in CG is assigned a new edge, it must be propagated to all its successors. Again, CG, by definition, is an acyclic graph.

Deletion of an edge (A, B) in CG is possible, only if there does not exist x and y such that $A(x)$ and $B(y)$ are true and there is no edge connecting x and y in ICG. This means that an edge in CG cannot be deleted as long as there are instance objects that participate in the relationship represented by that edge in CG.

For an edge (x, y) in ICG, $Generic(x)$ cannot be true. This means that generic objects cannot make references to constituent objects, as they do not have internal assemblies.

5.2 Interaction between GG and CG

The generalization and composition graphs impact upon each other, as some of the composition properties of a node in CG may be inherited from its super-types. Therefore, every time GG is updated, its effect on CG will have to be gauged and changes to it will have to be made accordingly. Also, any incremental update to CG requires a look-up of GG to determine whether it results in other updates in CG.

As has been mentioned in Chapter 3, we do not allow the composition and generalization graphs to contain a cycle. Thus, any incremental update of CG and GG must check for the creation of a cycle. In the following, algorithms for making insertions and deletions in CG and GG are given.

Procedure CGInsert

/* An edge (A, B) is to be inserted into CG. */

1.   Find all successors of node A in GG. Let these nodes be $\{X_1, X_2,.., X_n\}$.

2.   Find all successors of node B in GG. Let these nodes be $\{Y_1, Y_2,.., Y_m\}$.

3.   For each node $X_r \in \{A, X_1, X_2, .., X_n\}$ and each node $Y_s \in \{B, Y_1, Y_2, .., Y_m\}$, insert $(X_r, Y_s) \in \{A, X_1, X_2,.., X_n\} \times \{B, Y_1, Y_2, .., Y_m\}$ into CG.

4.   For each insertion, check for a cycle in CG. If a cycle is detected, then abort the transaction.

It should be noted that at the steps 1 and 2, partial transitive closures need to be computed.

Procedure CGDelete

/* An edge (A, B) is to be deleted from CG. */

1. Find all successors of node A in GG. Let these nodes be $\{X_1, X_2,.., X_n\}$.

2. Find all successors of node B in GG. Let these nodes be $\{Y_1, Y_2, .., Y_m\}$.

3. For each node $X_r \in \{A, X_1, X_2, .., X_n\}$ and each node $Y_s \in \{B, Y_1, Y_2, .., Y_m\}$, delete the edge $(X_r, Y_s) \in \{A, X_1, X_2,.., X_n\} \times \{B, Y_1, Y_2, .., Y_m\}$ from CG.

Procedure GGInsert

/* An edge (A, B) is to be inserted into GG */.

1. Insert (A, B) in GG.

1.1 Check for a cycle. If a cycle is detected, then abort the transaction.

2. Find all immediate successors of node A in CG.

3. For all nodes $\{X_1, X_2, .., X_n\}$ found in the step 2, insert (B, X_1), (B, X_2) .. (B, X_n) into CG by calling procedure CGInsert.

Procedure GGDelete

/* An edge (A, B) is to be deleted from GG. */

1. Find all immediate successors of node A in CG.

2. For all nodes $\{X_1, X_2 ,.., X_n\}$ found in the step 2, delete $(B, X_1), (B, X_2), .. (B, X_n)$ from CG by calling procedure CGDelete.

3. Delete (A, B) from GG.

5.3 Efficient Management of CG and GG

In the previous section, algorithms were outlined for managing the updates of GG and CG and the effects of these updates upon each other. In a design database, these graphs can be very large. Thus, it is essential that some technique should be devised that efficiently handles the update of GG and CG. For, this purpose we propose that the transitive closures of GG and CG be maintained. The motivation for doing so is manifold. First, as noted earlier, the algorithms for update require the computation of partial transitive closures. Second, insertion into the transitive closure relations can detect a cycle as a part of the algorithm; thus, the detection of cycles requires no extra work. Third, in design databases, the queries that involve the transitive closures of CG and GG are very frequent; hence, maintenance of transitive closure relations eliminates the overhead of computing it whenever such queries are posed.

However, the problem with maintaining the transitive closure of a graph is the storage requirement, which in the worst case can be $O(n^2)$. In the following section, a strategy for efficient storage of transitive closure relations is outlined. A performance analysis and storage requirement for this strategy are also discussed. On the basis of this performance analysis and the time complexities of known algorithms for computing transitive closure and for the detection of cycles, it is shown that maintenance of transitive closure results in a better performance in handling updates and answering queries.

5.3.1 Maintenance of Transitive Closure Relations

In this section, we give a compression scheme [Sch83, Agr89] for storing and maintaining the transitive closure of a directed acyclic graph. We also give algorithms for doing incremental deletion and update of transitive closure relations.

The compression scheme proposed here is a range compression. The basic idea is to assign numbers to nodes so that instead of individually listing all nodes within a certain range of values in a successor list the range could be recorded. In order to develop a technique that yields maximal compression, the given graph is covered with one or more spanning trees, and the tree is used to generate node numbers. In the case of a directed tree, each node is numbered to reflect its relative position in a postorder traversal of the tree. The number of the node is called its postorder number. After this numbering, each node is assigned an index consisting of the lowest postorder numbers among its successors. For simplicity, the index associated with a leaf node is the same as its postorder number.

The above scheme can be generalized for the case of a directed acyclic graph, which is assumed to have connected components. If there are disjoint components, they can be connected by creating a virtual root node. The compression scheme for a DAG is given below.

1. Find a spanning tree T for the given graph G.

2. Assign postorder numbers and indexes to the nodes of T. At the end of this step, an interval [i, j] is associated with each node, such that j is the postorder number of the node and i is the lowest postorder number among its successors.

3. Examine all the nodes of G in the reverse topological order. At each node p, do the following: (i) for every arc (p, q) add all the intervals associated with the node q to the interval associated with the node p; (ii) if the interval being added contains the postorder number of the node then there is a cycle; (iii) at the time of adding an interval to the interval set of a node, if one interval is subsumed by another, discard the subsumed interval.

After this processing, each node of the graph is associated with a unique interval that contains reachability information for the nodes that can be reached by following the tree arcs starting from this node. In addition, there are intervals associated with a node that provide reachability information for the nodes that can be reached by following one or more nontree arcs from this node. Figure 5-1 shows an example of a rooted DAG, where the reachability of each node is given by the labels associated with it. The solid arrows represent tree arcs, whereas dashed arrows signify nontree arcs. The first label for each node represents its reachability following the tree arcs emanating from it, whereas other labels give the information for its nontree arcs.

The complexity of computing the compressed transitive closure of a graph is the same as the computation of a transitive closure. Both are of $O(n^3)$ complexity in the worst case, where n is the number of nodes in the graph. However, compression is one-time activity, and once compressed closure has been obtained, it can be repeatedly used to efficiently answer queries.

For maintaining the transitive closure of a graph, it is essential that efficient algorithms be provided for doing incremental updates to the graph. Therefore, while assigning postorder numbers to the graph, it is not necessary to choose contiguous numbers; gaps can be left between numbers and the compression scheme will still work correctly. The initial gap could be determined by dividing the range of integers that will fit into a word by the expected number of nodes in the graph. Alternatively, real numbers could be used instead of integers.

In the following, we describe an algorithm for the insertion of an edge. Consider a new node j connected by a new arc (i, j) to be inserted at an existing node i. Note that there can never be a new node i for a new arc (i, j), as we are considering a DAG with a virtual root node.

1. Let the postorder number of i be n and that of its immediate successors with the smallest postorder number be m. If i is a leaf node, m is taken to be one less than the lowest number in the range of intervals associated with i. Find two postorder numbers between m and n that have already been assigned and have the largest difference. Let n_1 and n_2 be these numbers. Assign to j the postorder number $n_3 = (n_1 + n_2)/2$ and the interval $[n_1 + 1, n_3]$.

2. For the addition of a new nontree arc (i, j), the intervals associated with j will have to be added to node i and all its predecessors. If any of the intervals being added to a node contains its postorder number, then there is a cycle. Moreover, if the new interval is subsumed by an interval associated with the node, then this interval is discarded. If no new interval is added to a node, the effect is not propagated to its predecessor.

An algorithm for deleting an existing edge in a graph is described below. For the deletion of a node, all edges that have this node as a head or a tail are deleted.

1. For the deletion of a tree arc (i, j), take the subtree rooted at j and make it the child of the virtual root node, renumber the nodes in the subtree by assigning them numbers greater than L, which is the largest postorder number being currently used. The postorder number of the virtual node is assumed to be ∞. Update the tree intervals associated with the nodes in this subtree, but retain the nontree intervals.

2. Modify any nontree intervals that have old postorder numbers by new postorder numbers. (The new postorder numbers are created by renumbering the nodes of the subtree in the step 1.)

3. If any of the tree predecessor of j in the old graph had a nontree arc coming into node k of the subtree rooted at j, they inherit the intervals associated with k.

5.3.2 Complexity of Search, Deletion and Insertion

We present a time analysis of the algorithms given here for the maintenance of transitive closure relations. This analysis is based on a proposed data structure for the compression scheme that comprises a collection of list, each of which contains the node, the postorder numbers of its immediate successors, and a set of tree and nontree intervals associated with it. Other data structures will not change this analysis of algorithms.

Let n be the number of nodes in the graph and d be the average number of intervals associated with each node. Clearly, retrieval of transitive closure requires two passes. One for finding the predecessors or successors of the node; in the worst case, the cost of finding the successors is $O(n+d)$ and of finding the predecessors is $O(n*d)$. The other pass is needed for interpreting the postorder numbers of the retrieved node, which is of cost $O(n)$. Hence, the cost of retrieval, in general, is $O(n*d)$.

For the addition of a tree arc (i, j), the cost of search for i's immediate child with the smallest postorder number and two postorder numbers is $O(n)$. For the addition of a nontree arc, one pass is required for adding the intervals associated with j to i and all of its predecessors, which is $O(n*d)$. Hence, the cost of addition is $O(n*d)$.

For the deletion of an arc (i, j), the update of the tree intervals of the subtree rooted at j and the update of all relevant nontree intervals requires one pass and thus have $O(n*d)$ complexity. Two more passes are required to find the tree predecessors of i that has an arc coming to the subtree and for adding nontree intervals to these nodes; the costs of both these passes are $O(n*d)$. Hence, the cost of deletion is $O(n*d)$.

In the worst case, the average number of intervals associated with each node can be of $O(n^2)$. For instance, in a bipartite graph, the total number of interval required can be $(n+1)^2/2$. The worst case seems to occur when a large number of nodes have the same set of immediate successors. However, in such cases, a single common virtual node can be created as an intermediary. There will be only one interval associated with the virtual node and thus only one more interval will be added to all its predecessors. However, we do not expect worst case graphs to arise in the applications envisaged. In the ideal case when the given graph is a strict hierarchy, only *one* interval is associated with each node. Thus, the storage requirement for the transitive closure of a hierarchical graph is of $O(n)$.

As the maximum number of edges in a directed acyclic graph is $n(n-1)/2$, the storage requirement for its full transitive closure can be $O(n^2)$ in the worst case, where n is the number of nodes in the graph. The detailed simulation analysis by Agrawal et al. shows that for a general graph with nodes in the range of 500-1000, the storage requirement for a compressed transitive closure tends to be *half* of the storage requirement of the original graph when the average out-degree of nodes is between five and ten [Agr89]. The total storage required was computed as the numbers of successors at each node for the original and transitive closure graphs.

The reasons for the compressed closure requiring less storage than even the original graph are the following. As numbers of edges increase, a deeper, less branchy tree can be found to cover the graph. Most successors of a node can be reached through tree edges. Paths through nontree edges are mostly subsumed. A compressed closure also avoids the extra storage required for these "redundant" edges whose removal does not affect the reachability information in the graph.

It is clear from this storage requirement that d in most cases is less than $D/4$, where D is the average out-degree of nodes in the graph. The simulation analysis was done for arbitrary DAGs. It should be noted that graphs GG and, especially, CG contain hierarchical infrastructures, and thus d is expected to be quite small compared to D.

The data structure proposed in the scheme that contains both the original graph (i.e., the list of immediate successors) and the compressed transitive closure will require on average $(3s/2)$ storage, where s is the storage needed for the original graph.

5.3.3 Analysis of Time Complexity

Because of the consistency rule, the generalization and composition graphs are not allowed to have cycles. This means that at the time of every insertion in GG or CG a cycle detecting mechanism has to be used. The time complexity of detecting a cycle in a directed graph is $O(n + n*D)$, where n is the number of nodes and $n*D$ is the number of edges in the graph. The computations of transitive closure relations generaly involve $O(n^3)$ algorithms, though some techniques have been developed that give somewhat better performance than $O(n^3)$. As argued by Ioannidis and Ramakrishnan, only the semi-naive algorithm computes the partial transitive closure (i.e., the set of all predecessors or successors of a *given* node) efficiently, and it has $O(n + n*D)$ complexity [Ioa88]. With the exception of semi-naive algorithm, we must essentially compute the entire transitive closure first and then perform a selection.

We compare the time complexities of the algorithms given in Section 5.2 for two cases: (i) the transitive closure relation of GG and CG are maintained and (ii) their transitive closure relation are computed when required.

Consider procedure CGInsert. At the step 3, insertions take place; each insertion implies that creation of a cycle has to be checked. The cost of insertion in the case (ii) is $O(1)$, whereas the cost of detecting a cycle is an $O(n + n*D)$. In the case (i), the cost of insertion of an edge is $O(n*d)$. However, the detection of cycles is a part of the insertion algorithm with no extra cost. At the steps 1 and 2, partial transitive closures need to be computed. The semi-naive method can compute partial transitive closure in $O(n + n*D)$ time. In the case (i), the search to find a partial transitive closure (i.e., the successor list of the given node) is $O(n+d)$. Similar arguments can be made for procedure GGInsert, which calls procedure CGInsert. Thus, the maintenance of transitive closures improves the performance of insertion algorithms from $O(n + n*D)$ to $O(n*d)$. As d is expected to be quite small, we get a computational advantage of several factors.

The cost of deletion of an arc in the case (i) is $O(n*d)$ whereas its cost is $O(n)$ in the case (ii) for searching and deleting an arc. However, the steps 1 and 2 of procedure CGDelete compute partial transitive closure, which has been shown to have a better performance in the case (i). As d is expected to be small compared to D, the performance of deletion algorithms will still be better for case (i). Similar arguments can be made for GGDelete, which calls CGDelete.

It is clear that maintenance of the transitive closure relations of CG and GG provides less expensive updates and queries, though it has a higher storage requirement. The foregoing analysis shows that the trade-off it provides in terms of efficient performance far outweighs the storage requirement.

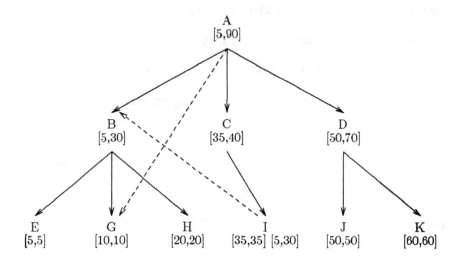

Figure 5-1

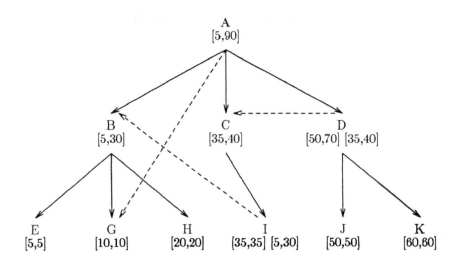

Figure 5-2

CHAPTER 6
A STORAGE STRATEGY FOR VERSIONED COMPOSITE OBJECTS

Design of a complex engineering object or a large software system is an intricate task. A design object may contain thousands of constituents, which can themselves have several versions. An efficient storage strategy for design objects is indispensable for keeping this task manageable. In this chapter, we propose a storage strategy for versioned composite objects, which involves clustering as well as indexing techniques for efficient retrieval, update and testing. The physical design of a database system requires that a number of decisions be made with respect to the parameters of the implemented system. A detailed knowledge of the system characteristics is required for a good design. However, this alone is not enough, since it is frequently the case that a group of parameters are so interrelated that changes in one requires adjustment in others in order to maintain a balanced design. The ostensible intractability of the problem perhaps explains why the work [Har87, Kim88, Ket88b] reported on storage strategies for composite objects does not take the dimension of versioning into consideration or deal with the frequent changes during the design phase.

The proposed storage strategy incorporates the expected design parameters—the structure, access and update pattern, versioning, and testing requirements of a design object. The underlying idea is to provide indexing facility for objects for direct retrieval and place them physically clustered on secondary storage so that disk access and page faults are minimized. The objective is to develop a database organization technique which supports efficient execution of frequent retrieval and update operations in CAD design databases.

74

6.1 Design Database Operations

In this section, we present an outline of a set of frequently occurring operations in a design database. These operations and their relative frequency and significance furnishes the basis of the proposed strategy. In the forthcoming discussion on composite instance graph, we use terms such as parent, child, descendent, ancestor, and sibling with obvious meanings from graph theory. We also use the term *twins* to refer to members in a version set.

The basic operation in a design database is the retrieval of an entire or partial design object, which is called *object retrieval (OR)*.

Other operations in design database normally require accessing objects that are interrelated to one another. The operations of accessing objects in a version set; that is, the transition from one twin to another is called *twin transition (TT)*.

An operation is needed in design databases to access all constituent objects of a given composite object. The operation of physical transition from one sibling constituent object to another is called *sibling transition (ST)*.

Other important operation in design databases is accessing constituent objects from their parent composite objects. Distinction must be made between this operation and the previously described operation ST. Here the transition is from a parent object to its first child object rather than between the siblings. This type of operation is called *parent-child transition (PCT)*.

Another important, though less frequent, operation is the access of all parent objects from a given child constituent object. Essentially, it is a transition from a child to its parents. This operation is called *child-parent transition (CPT)*. It should be noted that in the proposed versioning scheme a versioned object can be referenced by more than one objects, which belong to the same version set.

An operation is also needed which, given an object, provides access to all its constituents. This operation can be materialized by recursively applying the operation PCT. This operation is referred to as *ancestor-descendent transition (ADT)*. As argued in Chapter 5, this type of operation is quite frequently used in order to query a design at the template level. However, this operation at the instance level ceases to be very useful because of the huge amount of data retrieved.

6.2 Units of Clustering

Design objects are highly variable in size, as they have variable length and set-valued attributes. The storage subsystem required for design database must support heterogeneous and variable length records. Heterogeneous records imply that data pages in the storage subsystem contain different types of records. Variable length records mean that records of the same type are allowed to grow and shrink in size. The storage must also allow record clustering; that is, a new record can be stored in the vicinity of the specified storage location.

Most applications in design databases tend to retrieve a design object in its entirety or a large significant portion of it. Moreover, these retrievals tend to be object-oriented rather than set oriented [Ket88a]; that is, an object is retrieved given its object identifier, whereas in conventional databases a set of records is retrieved based on some criteria defined on their attributes. For the derivation operation (Section 4.3), an object is accessed in its entirety in order to create its copy. Therefore, records that belong to a design object must be physically collocated. An object constitutes an unpartitionable entity, and thus a fundamental unit of clustering.

In the following, we discuss the characteristics of design databases, which provide a strong motivation for a scheme that supports physical collocation of versions in a version set.

In an environment that supports versioning, a designer accesses different versions belonging to the same set in an exploratory manner for browsing and testing them, or for selecting them to be referenced as constituents, or for deriving a new version. As discussed in Section 4.2, all objects in a version set are equivalent and can be interchangeably referenced by a given composite object.

In the derivation operation, a version is created by copying a given version. The writing of the newly derived version is most likely to be stored on the same page as the source version. This minimizes page faults, as the page is expected to remain in buffer. By collocating all the versions of an object, the space can also be managed efficiently. The invariant attributes need not be replicated, as they are acquired from the generic object, which is also clustered with the versioned objets. A technique called delta refinement, which stores only the modified attribute values of a version, can be efficiently applied to the derived versions, if this scheme is supported.

The proposed model allows a composite object to make generic references to its constituents, which can be dynamically dereferenced by some default criteria. In generic reference no particular version is referenced and any object in the version set can be dynamically bound to its references. Therefore, by collocating versions in a set, the operations PCT and ST with generic references can be efficiently supported.

During the derivation phase, a new derived version can exist without being referenced by any parent object and thus may lead to dispersed storage. An example should illustrate this point. Consider a composite object A.v4 that references the object B.v2, which in turn references C.v5. Suppose a new version B.v3 is derived from B.v2. B.v3 also references the constituent object C.v5; however, A.v4's reference to B.v2 remains unchanged and for a period of time B.v3 can remain unreferenced. This implies that B.v3 must be collocated with its potential parents for efficient support of PCT and ST operations. It should be noted that B.v3 can be referenced in the future only by the versions belonging to the object A. Similar situation can also occur by frequent modifications of reference from one equivalent version to other. This scheme can eliminate the dispersed storage of related objects and efficient execution of TT, ST and PCT can be ensured.

The foregoing discussion attempted to demonstrate the necessity of physically clustering the members of a version set on the physical storage. This forms the second unit of clustering.

Identifying and accessing all the immediate constituents of a given object is an activity that occurs quite frequently in design databases. A composite object is defined in terms of its constituents. All constituents of a design objects are often accessed by the same transaction in order to explore them, or to examine whether they are complete and/or consistent, or to run validation test on them. This provides a motivation for storing sibling constituent objects close to one another on disk. This gives the third unit of clustering.

In Chapter 3, we gave some rules for building a composite object hierarchy. In Chapter 4, the basic requirements of versioning were discussed. It was observed that adding the dimension of versioning to a composite object hierarchy transforms it into a directed acyclic graph (DAG). Since in the versioning scheme, a constituent object can have more than one parent objects belonging to the same version set, the strict hierarchical property of ICG (Definition 2.12) is lost.

We noted earlier that TT and ST are frequently used operations in design databases. However, any traversal of a DAG cannot maintain the property of unintervened sequential access to all its child nodes, since a child node may belong to more than one parent and thus can be placed only in one set of siblings. A comparison of DAG and hierarchy traversals is discussed in the next section.

The principal insight underlying the proposed scheme is to transform a DAG into an equivalent hierarchy. This conversion is based on simple notions. First, we note that the nodes in the DAG have multiple parents, but they are at the same level. Second, all parents of a node must belong to the same version set; that is, they must be twins. Third, a node, though it may not currently have any parent and thus form a root in the DAG, can potentially acquire a parent only from a designated version set, which owns its twins. We have already argued the advantage of clustering the members of a version set; it should be pointed out that most of the twins are expected to be shared by the parent objects due to probative and derivative nature of design.

If all objects in a version set are treated as a single clustered node and the children of all objects in the set are treated as the children of the node, a DAG can be converted into a hierarchy. The following formalism gives a precise description of this transformation.

1. We observe that for any two edges (a, c) and (b, c) in the DAG, GenericInst(a) = GenericInst(b) always holds true.

2. For nodes $A_1, A_2, ..., A_k, ..., A_n$ in the DAG, there is a corresponding node A in the equivalent hierarchy, such that $A = \{ A_1, A_2, ..., A_k, ..., A_n \}$ and $\forall$ $A_i \in A$, GenericInst (A_i) has a unique value.

3. For any two nodes $A_i \in A$ and $B_j \in B$, if $\exists$ an edge (A_i, B_j) in the DAG, then there is an edge (A, B) in the equivalent hierarchy.

Figure 6-1 shows such a DAG. Figure 6-2 represents an equivalent hierarchy. In the hierarchy, A = {A.v1, A.v2}, B = {B.v1, B.v3, B.v4 }, D = { D.v3 }, N = { N.v1, N.v2 }, S = { S.v5}, etc. The edge (A, B) in the hierarchy corresponds to the DAG edges (A.v1, B.v4) and (A.v2, B.v3). Similarly, the edge (A, D) in the hierarchy corresponds to the edges (A.v1, D.v3) and (A.v2, D.v3), etc.

It should be pointed out the this transformation of a DAG into a hierarchy is motivated by a search for an optimum clustering. It provides arguably the most efficient sequential ordering of objects for the execution of design operations. The parent-child references in a DAG, which are represented in the internal assembly of an object, remain valid in their hierarchical representation.

6.3 Traversals of Hierarchies

In Section 6.1, we proposed a number of operations and three important units of clustering. The three operations——OR, TT, and ST——are fundamental to the nature of design databases. An efficient execution of these operations are provided by the proposed clustering and indexing (discussion of which is postponed to a later section) schemes. The operator PCT is also extremely important; in fact, the operation ST becomes meaningful only when it is preceded by a PCT. It is expected that there will be repeated calls to ST after a call has been made to PCT.

Therefore, the nodes of a hierarchy should be organized in a sequential order in which they are most likely to be accessed. Since any node can be directly accessed and thus can become a starting point in a sequential access to other nodes, the chosen pattern of organization must be recursively repeated. This is the sequential order in which nodes of a given hierarchy will be stored on disk. There are many ways a hierarchy can be traversed. Our goal is to find an optimal storage given the units of clustering and the expected frequency of the operations.

Any traversal of a hierarchy that provides a sequential order for storing its nodes must satisfy three requirements. First, a node must be visited before any of its descendents are visited; this ensures that the descendents of node can be accessed in a single, sequential forward traversal. Second, all children of a node must be collocated as close as possible. Third, any deletion and insertion in the existing hierarchy should produce a minimal restructuring of the sequential order. In design databases, an insertion does not necessarily apply to a single edge; a whole subtree representing an independent composite object can be inserted as a child of a node in another design hierarchy. This situation occurs when two composite object evolve independently and later one is referenced as a descendent by the other.

Depth-first and breadth-first traversals are two well-known methods for traversing a hierarchy. In depth-first traversal, a single branch of a hierarchy is traversed to the leaf level, and only then are other branches explored. In breadth-first traversal, a hierarchy is pursued one level at a time until it is fully traversed. These traversal methods are illustrated by the following examples. A hierarchy is shown in Figure 6-3. Assuming that child nodes of a given node are traversed from left to right, the following are the sequences in which depth-first and breadth-first traversals respectively visit the nodes of the hierarchy.

DFT: A B E H I J F G K L C M N D O Q R P

BFT: A B C D E F G M N O P H I J K L Q R

It is clear that both traversals meet the first criterion of accessing an ancestor node before accessing its descendents. However, depth-first traversal does not satisfy the second, and the most important, criterion of clustering the sibling nodes. Breadth-first traversal does not closely collocate child nodes with their parent.

Consider an independent design hierarchy shown in Figure 6-4, which is inserted as a subtree under node A in Figure 6-3; that is, α becomes another child node of A. The resulting hierarchy is shown in Figure 6-5 and its two traversals are given below.

DFT: A B E H I J F G K L C M N D O Q R P $\alpha \beta \delta \theta \gamma \mu \nu$

BFT: A B C D α E F G M N O P β ν H I J K L Q R δ θ μ ν

The above example illustrates that in depth-first traversal, the insertion of a subtree creates a minimal restructuring of the existing sequence, as the insertion is made at only one location. It is clear that the nodes belonging to the subtree are simply inserted at one point—that is, after the node P—without any restructuring of the sequence in the subtree. It should be pointed out that the insertion cannot always be at the end of the sequence. On the other hand, in breadth-first traversal, insertions are made at all levels that are common to both the hierarchies; that is, α must be inserted at the first level, and β and γ at the second level and so on. The subtree that is being inserted will have its nodes sequenced in the given order. The insertion in depth-first traversal utilizes this fact; however, the breadth-first traversal, due to its very definition, cannot; and, thus insertion for this case becomes very inefficient.

Consequently, neither of these traversals satisfies all the requirements of a design database. This has motivated us to devise a new method of traversal called *sibling-reverse-depth-first (SRDF)*, which is essentially a hybrid of the above two traversals. In SRDF traversal, once a node is visited, then all its child nodes are visited immediately. This procedure is recursively repeated in reverse order. The following procedural description defines the method in a more precise term.

```
Procedure SRDFT (A);
BEGIN
    Visit node A;
    IF node A has any children THEN
        BEGIN
            Visit all child nodes of A;
            For each child B of A
                Call SRDFT (B) in the reverse order;
        END;
END.
```

The sibling-reverse-depth-first traversal of the hierarchy shown in Figure 6-3 is given below.

SRDFT: A B C D O P Q R M N E F G K L H I J

In SRDF traversal, all children are visited immediately after a parent node is visited in order to impose a sequential clustering on the siblings; this is followed by a recursive application of this traversal on the child nodes in the reverse order; that is, the child that was visited last is chosen for the access of its descendents first. This ensures that for at least one node of each set of siblings, the descendents can be accessed without any intervening nodes. The SRDF traversal, as can be easily seen, meets the first and the second criteria. The idea behind this traversal is that if after having visited all child nodes, a designer accesses a descendent of the given node, then he/she is most likely to visit all the descendents of a child node before switching to the descendents of some other sibling node. Therefore, this traversal imitates the depth-first traversal to some extent. To investigate the effect of an insertion, the SRDF traversal of the resulting hierarchy is given below after the above mentioned insertion.

SRDFT: A B C D $\alpha \beta \gamma \mu \nu \delta \theta$ O P Q R M N E F G K L H I J

In SRDF traversal, an insertion of a subtree produces a minimal restructuring of the existing sequential order of a stored hierarchy. The subtree is already stored in SRDF sequence and its sequential order remains intact; the insertion takes place at a single location in the existing hierarchy. Therefore, the proposed SRDF traversal appears to be comparatively better than the two traversal schemes, as it meets all the three requirements. In the following, we give an insertion algorithm for SRDF traversal and show its correctness. The algorithm gives the procedure for inserting a subtree rooted at B under node A of a hierarchy rooted at R. The insertion preserves the three properties discussed earlier. The subtree is assumed to be ordered in SRDF sequence.

```
Procedure Insert_SRDF (R, A, B);
    BEGIN
        IF A has no child and A = R  THEN
            Insert the subtree rooted at B after A;
        IF A has one or more children  THEN
            Insert the entire subtree rooted at B immediately
                after the last child of A;
        IF A has no child and A ≠ R  THEN
            Find parent P of A and insert the subtree rooted
                at B immediately after the last child of P;
    END.
```

To show the correctness of the above algorithm, we observe that the insertion was required to be made at only one location. Hence, the third criterion is satisfied. To show that SRDF insertion algorithm ensures that all children are placed after the parent without any intervening nodes between the siblings, we consider each of three conditional statements in the algorithm. In the simplest case, when A has no children and it is a root node, the subtree rooted at B is inserted after A and thus B, the only child of A, follows A. If A has existing children, then the subtree rooted at B is placed immediately after the last child of A; thus B follows A and it is stored next to its sibling without any intervening node. Furthermore, the subtree does not intervene between other siblings of B, as it is inserted *after* all its siblings. Similarly, if A has no child but has a parent, then B is inserted immediately after all the children of A's parent, and the same argument as above applies. However, it should be pointed out that for efficient insertion the subtree is not inserted in the reverse order of the descendents of A's siblings, but simply inserted after all its siblings. This nonetheless maintains the SRDF sequence. To show that this insertion algorithm maintains the sequence of the descendent of any given node unintervened by any nodes that are not the descendent of the given node, it is observed that the insertion preserves the clustering sequence of siblings and since the descendents of B in the subtree are already in the desired sequence of SRDF, the property is maintained for the resulting sequence after an insertion.

Several types of deletion can occur in a design database. At the outset, it should be recalled that in the proposed model child objects are not considered existentially dependent on their parent (Rule 3.6); therefore, a deletion of a node does not require the deletion of its descendents.

A deletion of an edge in the original DAG for versioned objects does not require a deletion of any object in the hierarchy except for the modification of the reference. As explained before, an unreferenced object in version set does warrant its deletion or any restructuring.

Deletion of a versioned object calls for its removal from the version set and the deletion of all the references from its parent and child objects.

A deletion of an edge in the hierarchy of a composite object requires a restructuring of the stored sequence on disk. This deletion of an edge implies that the version set of a composite object completely discards the generic and specific references to its child object. In this case, the subtree representing the child object must be removed from the hierarchical sequence and be stored as a root object at some different location. This type of deletion is expected to rarely occur in design database. The deletion algorithm is given below; R is the root of the existing hierarchy and B is the root of the subtree being removed.

```
Procedure Delete_SRDF (R, B);
    BEGIN
        Locate the parent A of the node B;
        IF A has no child other than B and A = R  THEN
            Remove A and store it at a different location;
            {There is a new hierarchy rooted at B}
        IF A has no child other than B and A ≠ R  THEN
        BEGIN
            Remove B and all its descendents from the given
                hierarchy and store them at a new location;
            Restructure the original hierarchical sequence;
        END;
```

```
        IF A has more than one child  THEN
        BEGIN
               Remove B and all its descendents, restructure them
                   and store them contiguously at a new location;
               Restructure the original hierarchical sequence;
        END;
END.
```

The first three steps are straight-forward and need no explanation. In the last step, the removed subtree rooted at B needs to be restructured, as B and its descendents may not be contiguous. Deletion can leave the original hierarchy or the removed subtree in a state where its nodes are not stored contiguously on disk. Restructuring refers to their rearrangement in contiguously allocated pages.

6.4 Physical Organization of Composite Objects

In order to present a detailed description of the physical organization of composite objects, specific assumptions regarding the characteristics of the underlying storage manager must be made. Therefore, we limit ourselves to giving only an overview of the basic requirements for implementing the proposed clustering strategy.

We envision a paging environment, where storage space is partitioned in a number of fixed-size pages. We also assume that the storage manager provides a facility for linear address space, called chunk here. A chunk is a collection of contiguous set of pages. It is useful for grouping clusters together. The storage manager should provide a mechanism for sequential scan through all objects in a chunk, so that related objects can be placed in a common chunk. Since pages in a chunk are contiguous, it can provide support for objects that are required to be collocated on disk.

For each object, the following information is maintained: (oid, object-properties, children-pointer-array, parent-oid). The object-properties refer to external features and internal assembly properties described in Chapter 3. The children pointer array is an array of records that contain two fields: oid of the child object and its physical address. It is assumed that the values in the children-pointer-array are arranged in the order of their position in the clustering sequence. In the case of generic reference, the oid and address of the generic object is stored. The value in the parent-oid is the oid of the generic object for its parents.

A hierarchy represents a composite object——which forms its root——and all its descendents. Unrelated composite objects constitute independent hierarchies. We consider it extremely important that direct access should be provided to all objects. Thus we envision a B+ tree index structure that provides such access. The leaf pages of this B+ tree will contain the oid of the objects, and two pointer fields, which contain the physical address of the object and its version set (generic object).

We discussed three units of clustering: the object, the version set, and the set of siblings. The groups of objects that can be collocated on a single page or a chunk is heavily contingent upon the average size of objects, the page size, and the maximum number of pages allocated in a chunk. Ideally, the whole hierarchy or at least the objects in third group could reside on the contiguous pages of a chunk. For efficiency purposes, a set of pages must be exclusively reserved for a version set. All versions in a version set are collocated on these set of pages. The generic object for the set precedes the versioned object, which can be stored in the order they are created. Thus, starting from the generic object, the versions in the set can be sequentially scanned. A page table is reserved on the page where a generic object resides; this page table contains information about the version set such as its derivation graph, the protocol for determining the default version, its parent object, etc.

The requirement for the complete contiguity of pages for groups of clustered objects is quite reasonable [Car86, Hae87, Ket88b]. However, contiguity deteriorates due to dynamic object growth, creation of new versions and modification of constituent object references. Thus the storage manager must allow for dynamic reorganization of of storage clusters.

There are several well-known techniques, which can be used in order to enhance contiguity and minimize the cost of restructuring. The use of relative page number, offset in the pointer address, for referencing inside a storage cluster can minimize the cost of updating the pointers, when a data page is moved from one location to another. The only reorganization cost is updating the corresponding page table entries; all internal pointers remain valid. Even when a group of objects cannot completely reside on consecutive pages on disk, the allocation policy should attempt to minimize the physical distance between pages of the corresponding cluster. An efficient reorganization of clustered groups remains an important research area.

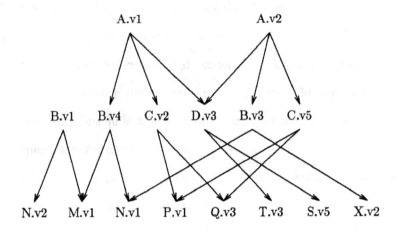

Figure 6-1

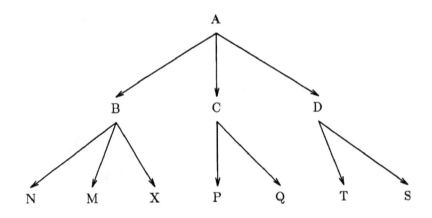

Figure 6-2

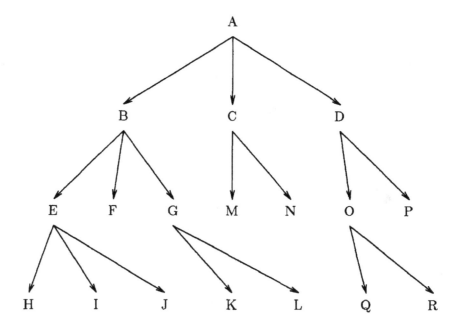

Figure 6-3

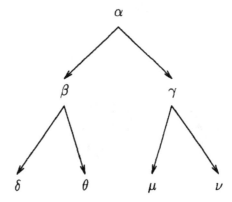

Figure 6-4

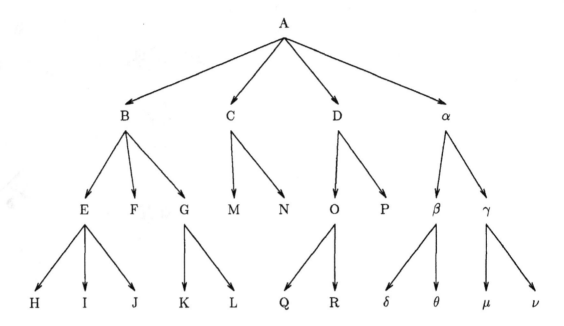

Figure 6-5

CHAPTER 7
DESIGN IN A COOPERATIVE CAD ENVIRONMENT

The objective of this chapter is to generalize the ideas discussed in Chapter 4 and describe protocols for maintenance, evolution, and validation of versions for a distributed CAD environment. Design is usually a result of integrated efforts of a group of designers. The nature of data sharing in design applications is different from conventional databases. The schema of design objects and validated versions are shared by databases of several design projects. The data in a design project are shared by the designers of the project. The design versions being experimented with and manipulated by a designer should not be shared by other designers. Moreover, a designer may begin a transaction which involves large amounts of data and may persist for a long period of time. Consequently, transaction in design applications cannot be considered as a unit of recovery, as in conventional databases management systems, interference among concurrent transaction is avoided by locking and timestamping. However, conventional techniques for transaction management cannot be used in design applications, as the volume of data involved and the duration of transactions are considerably greater.

To allow consistent versioning of design objects, to provide an efficient and secure transaction management, to manage large numbers of complex constraints involved in design databases, and to provide an environment conducive to sharing, evolution and testing of design objects, we propose a system architecture for design environment. The architecture for CAD databases is often envisioned as a a collection of hierarchically organized private, project and public databases [Cho86, Buch85]. Versions of different characteristics and capabilities reside in different databases. As design objects are hierarchically formed of other design objects, the constituent objects of a design object may reside in different databases and may have different statuses. Therefore, when a constituent object that references it is modified or deleted, the composite object must be notified of the change. In the following sections, we give the details of the proposed architecture and describe protocols for change notification.

7.1 A CAD Architecture

The proposed CAD architecture comprises four types of databases called data dictionary, public database, project database and private database. This architecture is essentially hierarchical as illustrated in Figure 7-1. Different design databases contain data under different characteristics. The logical and physical division is based on the accessibility and stability of design data and the types of operations performed on them. In Chapter 4, we outlined three classes of version states: validated, stable, and transient. In a distributed environment, versions with different states reside in different databases. This reduces the overhead of their management and enhances their independent evolution, shareability and testing. The next four sections describe the distinguishing functions and features of these databases.

7.1.1 Data Dictionary

Data dictionary contains the information about the meta data —schema, data definitions, constraints—as well as control of database such as the information about Checkout and Checkin and change-notification protocols. It is managed by a central database server, which also coordinates the sharing of data among different databases.

Schema and data definitions of a design object normally originate from private databases and after approval and verification by their project database, they are passed on to the data dictionary, where they permanently resides. This is shown in Figure 7-1, an arrow represents the direction of data flow. The schema is not allowed to be modified or deleted in the data dictionary, as long as its version instances exist in some database. To allow incremental design, external features (EF) and internal assembly (IA) functions can be defined in two separate stages. A design object can be referenced as a constituent object, if its external features have been defined. As mentioned in Chapter 2, IA and EF belong to different classes; hence different constraints can be imposed on them. Therefore, this incremental design strategy is *not* considered a schema modification.

It is not possible to create version instances of a design object whose data definition is not in the data dictionary. In other cases, modification and deletion is allowed if authorized by the database administrator.

7.1.2 Public Database

A Public database is universally accessible, and is characterized by the approved design data it contains. Approved design data include unversioned and validated versioned objects. This may also include a part library of simple design objects. The public database is also managed by a central database server. Various projects, after a successful series of testing and verification of their stable versions, promote and transfer them to validated versions into the public database by the Checkin operation (Section 7.3).

Validated versions, as defined in Section 4.2.2, are not allowed to be updated or deleted. It is also required that all design objects that are referenced by validated versions must also exist in the public database. This implies that a validated version can make reference to only unversioned and other validated versioned objects. The reason for this constraint is that transient versions can be derived in project databases from validated versions; if this constraint is not imposed, a design object can reference versions in databases to which it is not allowed to have direct access.

The public database contains immutable, completed and validated design objects, which can be used by other design objects. This scheme provides efficient browsing and retrieval operations.

7.1.3 Project Database

Project databases serve as a repository of *stable* versioned objects, which are experimented with and shared by the designers of the project. The final phase of testing and validation is performed in project databases by the project administrator. After successful testing, a stable version can be promoted and transferred to the public database as a validated version. Sophisticated constraint management, application programs, simulations, and concurrency control systems are needed for project databases.

The designers of a project, working in their private databases, can share and access data residing in the project database. They can copy a version residing in the project database to their private databases by a Checkout operation, modify and test it, and reinstall it to the project database by the Checkin operation. A project database, however, is not accessible to other designers, as shown in Figure 7-1.

A version is called complete (Definition 2.12), if all its references are bound to constituent objects that reside in databases accessible from it. Versioned objects in a project database must not be incomplete.

It is required that all versions referenced by a stable version in a project database must be either stable or validated and must reside in the same database or in the public database. This scheme ensures that a checked-out version (from a project database) in a private database does not reference objects residing in databases that are not accessible from it.

A stable version residing in a project database is essentially unmodifiable. However, as explained in Section 4.2.1, equivalence modifications are allowed on its internal assembly; its nonversion-significant attributes can also be modified. The object can be deleted. Modifications and deletions are privileged operations and can be performed only by an authorized designer. Since simulation and testing are performed in project databases, a stable version can be required to be deleted, if it does not meet certain specification or predefined constraints. Versions that reference the deleted version can become incomplete, if they also reside in the project database, since a stable version in a project database must have all its references bound to objects in the same database or validated versions in the public database. In such cases, the project administrator can use replacement modification, if an object in the version set of the deleted version resides in the accessible databases; otherwise, all the referencing versions must also be deleted.

In certain circumstances, a project database is also allowed to contain validated versions, if their replicas (defined in Section 7.2) also exist in the public database. The situation that warrants this and the protocol to handle it are discussed in Section 7.2. In such cases, a validated version can be deleted from the project databases.

7.1.4 Private Database

Designers perform much of the design and the bulk of verification and testing in private databases, which runs on work stations. A private database has direct access only to the data dictionary and its project database. The direction of data flow should be noted in Figure 7-1. The design objects in a private database are accessed and owned by one user. They are not accessible to other designers. A private database interfaces with other designers of the project through its project database.

Data retrieval, data definition and data manipulation and constraint management facilities are required in private databases. There is no need for concurrency control because these are single user databases.

Private database contain both transient and stable versions. Here, a designer can create new versions, derive versions from existing versions, promote transient versions to stable status, and check in stable versions to its project database, and check out copies of versions residing in its project and the public databases. All design objects referenced by versions in a private database must reside in the same private database, its project database or the public database.

Interface values of a generic object can be modified in a private database, only if it resides in the database of its origin, is not referenced by other objects, and the modification does not affect the internal assembly of stable versions. In all other cases, interface is considered invariant, as its modification can render all objects that reference it invalid. Schema and data definitions, as mentioned earlier, are also defined in a private database.

7.2 Operations on Versions in Distributed Environment

In Chapter 4, we defined several operations on versions such as version creation, derivation and promotion. In this section, we define high level operations in terms of these operations for the distributed CAD environment.

Checkout is defined as a derivation from a stable or validated version residing in a project or public database and installing it as a transient version in the private database that invoked the operation. It should be noted that the Checkout operation can be invoked only from a private database to the public database or its project database. Long transactions are not needed in this case, since it is a read-only operation.

Checkin is defined as transferring and installing a version from a less accessible database to a more accessible database. Thus, by definition, only stable versions can be transferred to a project database and validated versions can be transferred to the public database from project databases. A Checkin operation is not valid unless the version being checked in the new database can access all the versions it references.

RCheckin is defined as a Checkin preceded by a replication of the version being transferred to some other database. Replication in this case implies creation of an exact replica of the version. These two versions are identical and have the same object identifier and the same version number. To maintain the correspondence between the two replicas, some new functions need to be defined on type *Version*. Following functions can be defined.

function Db_Address (Version) = db_id;
function R_Address (Version) = db_id;

The function Db_Address returns the database where the version originated and the function R_Address indicates the database where its replica exists; a null address will signify the nonexistence of a replica. The db_id stands for database identifiers, which is unique and is assigned to each database. It is assumed that every private database generates object identifier unique across all project/public databases, which can preclude possible future conflicts.

The concept of replicas is extremely important in a distributed design environment. Design is a matter of team effort, which goes through several phases of testing and validation. A designer who needs direct access to a version that referenced by versions in the private database and still wants to allow other designers to experiment with it can use RCheckin operation. The disadvantage with deriving other version from it and using Checkin operation is that the IA properties of the versions that reference it have to be reassigned. Moreover, its version in the project database can be modified. An example should illustrate the point. Consider a private database that has a versioned object A.v1 that references a constituent object B.v3 in the same database. B.v3 is a stable version and the designer would like the version to be shared by designers on the project; however, it is also needed for the tests being run on A.v1. If replicas are not allowed, the only alternative is to derive a version B.v4 (say) from B.v3, promote it to stable status and invoke Checkin operation to install it in the project database. However, when the designer is done with the testing, he/she has to delete B.v3 and modify the references to B.v3 by B.v4 in A.v1. However, there is no guarantee that B.v4 exists and that it has not been modified. If a replica is allowed, the designer can delete its replica in the private database without having to update the references in A.v1, as replicas have the same object identifier and the same version number. This also guarantees that the B.v3 replica remains unmodified. This strategy reduces considerable overhead and make testing more efficient.

Existence of a replica precludes updates of any kind on it. Therefore, modification is disallowed on versions with replica. This provides a facility for ensuring that a version is not modified in the project database. If a modification is considered essential in the private database, a new version can be derived from it and modifications can be incorporated there. Any version that resides in a private or project database can be deleted. A deletion of a version that has been replicated requires a notification to its replica. Notification protocol is the topic of a subsequent section. A Checkin operation will also be disallowed on versions with a replica, as it is redundant.

Three new operations were defined in this section that were based on some of the operations defined earlier. We summarize the functions and scopes of these operations.

1. Versions can be created from scratch in a private database. These versions are transient.

2. A transient version can be promoted to a stable status in a private database.

3. A transient version can be derived from a stable version residing in the same private database.

4. A transient version can be derived in a private database from a stable version that resides in its project database.

5. A transient version can be derived in a private database from a validated version that resides in a project or the public database.

6. A stable version can be promoted to a validated status in a project database.

7. A stable version in a private database can be transferred to the project database as a stable version by the Checkin operation.

8. A validated version in a project database can be transferred to the public database by the Checkin operation.

9. A replica of a stable version in a private database can be transferred to the project database by RCheckin operation.

10. A replica of a validated version in a project database can be transferred to the public database by Checkin operation.

Table 7-1 summarizes the operations allowed on versions with different states and residing in different databases. The table shows the constraints under which a particular operation can be invoked, rather than the outcomes of invoking the operation.

7.3 Dynamic and Static Bindings in the Multilevel Environment

In section 4.3, we discussed static and dynamic bindings in the context of a single database. In this section, we extend the notions of dynamic and static binding (also called generic and specific references) for the proposed distributed architecture.

Rules of static binding are straightforward. All the specific references of a design object must be in the databases that are accessible from the location where it resides; for instance, a version in a private database can reference versions in the same private database, its project database and the public database irrespective of the statuses of versions. The only exception is for validated versions in a project database, which can reference other validated versions only, since a version cannot be characterized as validated unless all its constituents have been validated.

The case of dynamic binding, however, presents a problem. It is stipulated that validated versions do not contain any generic references. Its reasons will shortly become clear. The generic references in a stable version can use different criteria for dereferencing their default versions during their testing and validation phase; but before a stable version can be promoted to validated status, all its generic references must be converted to appropriate specific references. Stable and transient objects are allowed to contain generic references. Different default criteria can be maintained in different databases for version sets belonging to a generic object. The priority for dereferencing a dynamic binding using different default criteria will depend upon the accessibility of the database; that is, the dereferencing of a dynamic binding in an object residing in a private database must use the default criteria of that database; if that fails, it approaches its project and then the public database for their default criteria.

Different versions of a generic object reside in various databases, which may not have direct access to one another. This implies that different subsets of a version graph will be stored in these databases. Moreover, associated with each of these subsets of a version graph, there is a default mechanism for dereferencing a generic reference.

In view of the three operations defined in Section 7.2, the following strategy is proposed. In each database the version graph contains the versions that reside in the database and their parent version from which they were derived. Since a version can be derived through a Checkout operation from version residing in project databases, the parent of a version in the version graph of private database may not exist there. Moreover, different versions of a generic object can be derived independently in different private databases, there can be a conflict in version numbers at the time of Checkin to a project and the public database, which must have capability to resolve this. Deletion of a version should not lead to its deletion from a version graph; version graphs, as they represent the version derivation history, should only flag that version as nonexistent. The union of all subsets of version sets should provide the complete version graph of a generic object.

7.4 Requirements for Notification

In our model, a design object can be referenced by more than one version of its composite objects, which can reside in different databases and can have different statuses. Therefore, a change notification must be issued to the affected databases so that appropriate actions can be taken, when constituent objects are updated or deleted. It should be noted that modification and deletion can take place both in private and project databases. Following instances of update and deletion require change notification.

1. When one version belonging to a pair of stable replicas is deleted in a private or a project database, the other database is notified so that the value of function R_Address in the other version can be updated to signify that its replica no longer exists. This frees it from the restriction of no update.

2. When one version belonging to a pair of validated replicas is deleted in a project or the public database, the other database is notified so that the function R_Address in the other version can be updated to signify that its replica no longer exists.

3. When a replicated version is checked in the public database from a project database, a notification is sent to the private database of its origin so that the R_Address of its replica can be modified.

4. A version residing in a private database references, generically or specifically, an unreplicated version in its project database. When such a constituent version is deleted, the private database is notified of this change so that the affected version can update its references.

5. A version residing in a private database references, generically or specifically, a version in its project database. When such a constituent version is updated, the private database is notified of this change so that the the designer can review the references of the affected objects.

6. A stable version residing in a project database references a version in the same database. When such a constituent version is updated, the affected versions is notified of this change so that the designer can review the references of the affected objects.

7. A stable version residing in a project database references an unreplicated version in the same database. When such a constituent version is deleted, the affected version must be deleted as it becomes inconsistent. (A version is considered unreplicated in this context, if its replica exists only in a private database.)

However, if deletion is preceded by a replacement modification, then the cases 4 and 5 apply.

In Cases 1, 2, 3 and 4, notifications must be sent, which initiate an update. For the cases 5 and 6, an update is not necessary, but the designer of the object must be aware of the changes in the constituents of its design objects. Therefore, following the literature, we propose message-based and flag-based notifications.

In the message-based notification, which is required for the cases 1, 2, 3 and 4, the system will send a message to notify the change to appropriate databases (designers) of the affected versions. In the cases 1, 2 and 3, the database address of the replica is contained by the other version, thus it can be notified. The case 4 presents a problem, as a design object may be referenced by versions of the same object residing in different private databases; and the reference can be either generic or specific. On the other hand, in this model, the boundary of an object has been delineated so that objects that reference a constituent object are not logically a part of that referenced object. A simple solution would be to notify all the private databases, which belong to the project database. The other solution would be to query the data dictionary that contains the information about Checkout/Checkin and notify those private databases that contain versions which references the deleted object.

For the cases 5 and 6, as mentioned in Section 4.1, no update is necessary. Therefore, the notification is proposed to be flag-based. For flag-based notification, every version has the following functions defined on it.

function Creation_Time (Version) = Timestamp;
function Modification_Time (Version) = Timestamp;
function Verification_Time (Version) = Timestamp;

The function Creation_Time, as described earlier, represents the time when the version was created; the function Modification_Time represets the time it was last modified; and the function Verification_Time represents the time when it was verified whether it was reference consistent by checking the modification times of its constituents. A version X is considered *reference consistent*, if for all versions Y which it references, the following holds true.

$$\text{Verification\_Time (X)} > \text{Modification\_Time (Y)}$$

Thus, a designer is expected to periodically check if a design object is reference consistent or not. The designer then decides whether the object needs to be modified. In any case, he/she can set the verification time as the current time. When an object makes generic references, modification times of its dynamically bound constituents are not relevant. It should be noted that stable and transient versions are allowed to be version inconsistent. Validated versions, by definition, are always reference consistent; therefore, they are not allowed to have generic references.

In this chapter, we presented an architecture for a CAD database. It provided a unifying framework for incorporating the distributed nature of CAD databases, the configuration of complex objects, and different versions, which have different statuses, of a design object. A set of of protocols was proposed to manage change in the distributed environment. Changes in different databases require that affected databases be notified. Two notification techniques and its concomitant functions were also discussed. The foregoing approach was based on the model of composite objects and version concepts proposed in previous chapters.

Central Database Server

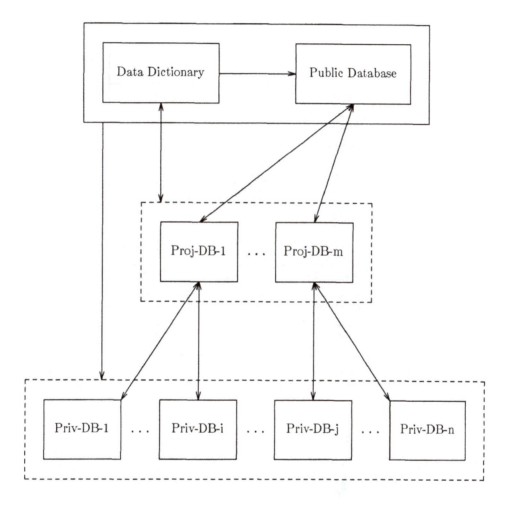

Figure 7-1

Object	Database Type	Operation
Transient	Private	Promote
Stable	Private	Derive
Generic	Private	Create
Stable	Private	Checkin
Stable	Private	Rcheckin
Stable	Project	Promote
Stable	Project	Checkout
Validated	Project	Checkout
Validated	Project	Checkin
Validated	Project	Rcheckin
Validated	Public	Checkout

Table 7-1

CHAPTER 8
CONCLUSION

8.1 Major Results

In this dissertation, a number of important concepts have been proposed for defining a unifying framework for the effective management of design data. In our view, the major results and contributions of this work are the following.

The dissertation introduced a formal treatment and the basic features of an object-oriented data model. We consider it important that our solutions to the problems of version management be developed within an underlying data model for design databases. This furnished a criterion to judge the correctness and feasibility of these solutions.

The classification of composite object attributes, enforcement of update constraints through the notion of class, the concepts of generic objects, invariant attributes, value acquisition, the mechanism for control of version proliferation and for interrelating disparate types of objects are some of the contributions made in the area of version management.

The next logical step was to generalize these ideas and demonstrate their applicability in a shared and cooperative design environment. A justification for a multi-level, distributed CAD architecture was given and protocols for version sharing, replication, validation and change-notification were discussed.

The last two chapters addressed some implementation-oriented issues. In these chapters, our main concern was to formulate techniques, which can be utilized for efficiently retrieving and organizing the schema and the extension of design data.

It was observed that the generalization and composition graphs, interdepend upon each other. The analysis of the algorithms developed for maintaining consistency demonstrated an enhanced performance when stored, rather than the dynamically computed, transitive closure of these graphs are used. The trade-off it provides far outweighs the space requirement of the interval labeling technique for transitive closure relations.

The problem of an efficient organization of design data, with its hierarchical structure compounded by the versioning dimension, was ostensibly intractable. We presented a detailed scheme that determines an optimal storage organization based on significant units of clustering and expected frequency of retrieval and update operations.

This dissertation presented well-defined formalisms, which provide consistent and coherent paradigms for version management in design databases.

8.2 Future Research Directions

In this section, we point out the directions for the future research in this area. There are several issues in computer-aided design, which have not attracted much attention from the investigators.

First of these issues is transaction management in design databases. The conventional model of transaction is based on the notions of serializability and atomicity. This model has served conventional data processing application well. However, it is not applicable to CAD environment. Transactions in a CAD environment are of long duration and represent interactive modifications to a complex design. A CAD environment requires a significantly different model of transaction, as it must allow a group of cooperating designers to arrive at a design without waiting over long duration. Thus, a model of CAD transactions are needed to support a design environment that involves a group of designers. The distributed architecture proposed in Chapter 5 can serve as a basis database for future transaction models. Recovery schemes and concurrency control techniques are also needed for CAD environment.

Second of these problems is the development of a space efficient technique for storing a version set. In Chapter 7, we alluded to a *delta* or *differential* scheme. In this scheme, only the modified parts of versions are stored; to materialize a version object, its previous version and its delta are used. An investigation for developing well-defined implementation techniques appears quite important.

Another issue is the formulation of a query language for versioned and composite objects. Little attention has been devoted to defining appropriate semantics for querying composite aggregation hierarchies and multiple representations of objects. This reluctance perhaps stems from the inherent difficulty of conventional query languages to express queries that involve recursively defined constructs. This query language will be able to support transitive closure as part of a facility for manipulating recursive structures. Thus, an enhanced query language is required, which would deal with the dimension versioning and provide a user-friendly interface for efficiently retrieving data.

APPENDIX
AN EXAMPLE OF VERSIONING PROCESS

In this appendix, we provide a simple example of the design of a composite object which goes through a process of versioning. For the sake of convenience, the example chosen here is based on the composite object *Adder* and its constituents discussed in Chapter 3. The idea behind this example is to illustrate the concepts and methodologies proposed in Chapter 4.

We mentioned in Chapter 3 that our model is not restricted to either top-down or bottom-up design strategies. In fact, any combination of these strategies are allowed. The design example given here evolves using an arbitrary combination of both of these strategies.

We establish a convention for identifying different objects. A type object always appears in lower-case italics with a suffix of "bb" or "wb"; "bb" signifies the fact that it represents the black-box properties whereas "wb" corresponds to white-box properties. An instance object appears with its first letter capitalized with a suffix of "G" or "V.*"; "G" signifies a generic object whereas "V.*" stands for a versioned object (where * can be any ordinal number).

Let us consider the design of the composite object Adder (Figures 3-2 and 3-3). In this example, a designer starts with a high level (external features) description of this object by declaring its type and functions that belong to its external features; at a later stage of design, its internal assemblies can be defined. The type and its functions are defined as follows.

User_Type: *adderbb*;

function ADName $(adderbb)$ $\longrightarrow$ $charstring$ u

function Designer $(adderbb)$ $\longrightarrow$ $charstring$

function ADInput $(adderbb)$ $\longrightarrow$ $terminal$ u, m

function ADOutput $(adderbb)$ $\longrightarrow$ $terminal$ u, m

The above functions define Name, Design, and interface of the type object of Adder. The user-defined type has no supertype or subtype at this stage. The functions declared here belong to different classes. Thus, they must be categorized as such.

$\{ \text{ADName} \} \in D_S{}^1$

$\{ \text{Designer} \} \in D_S{}^2$

$\{ \text{ADInput, ADOutput} \} \in I_F$

$D_S{}^1$ and $D_S{}^2$ stand for descriptive attributes and I_F stands for interface properties. It should be noted that different constraints can be imposed on the updatability of the function classes I_F, $D_S{}^1$, $D_S{}^2$, IA, etc. Functions declared as instances (members) of these classes inherit those constraints and thus can characterize *invariant, version-significant,* and *nonversion-significant* properties of objects. The interrelationship between these classes of functions and the above-mentioned three categories are illustrated in Figures 4-2, 4-3, and 4-4.

Now the designer can declare an object instance of type *adderbb*, which can be designated as a generic object by declaring it as an instance of type *Generic.*

AddInstance AderG to type *adderbb*;

AddInstance AderG to type *Generic*;

AderG is a surrogate for an instance of *adderbb*. This is also a generic object. Having created Adder1, the designer can now "instantiate" its functions as follows. (Instantiation of functions here refers to providing their range and domain values.)

ADName (AdderG) := "Adder";

ADOutput (AdderG) := { Z1, Z2, Z3, Z4, Z5 };

ADInput (AdderG) := { X1, X2, X3, X4, Y1, Y2, Y3, Y4 }.

These function instantiations refers to Figure 3-2. Here we have made the assumption that the type *terminal* and its above instances have already been declared.

The designer can use this generic object as a constituent of any other composite object. The point that must be emphasized is that the generic object AdderG can participate in higher level objects, although its internal design is not yet complete.

To build the internal assembly of AdderG, the designer realizes that he needs an object called Adder Slice (shown in Figure 3-4). The declaration of this object is done as follows:

User-Type: adderslicebb;

function ASName (*adderslicebb*) $\rightarrow$ *charstring* u

function Designer (*adderslicebb*) $\rightarrow$ *charstring*

function ASInput (*adderslicebb*) $\rightarrow$ *terminal* u, m

function ASOutput (*adderslicebb*) $\rightarrow$ *terminal* u, m

{ ASName } $\in D_S^{1}$

{ ASInput, ASOutput } $\in I_F$

An instance of type *adderslicebb* is created below.

AddInstance AdderSliceG to type *adderslicebb*;

AddInstance AdderSliceG to type *Generic*;

Its functions can be instantiated as follows.

ASName (AdderSliceG) := "Adder-Slice";

ASInput (AdderSliceG) := { X, Y, CI };

ASOutput (AdderSliceG) := { Z, CO };

These function instantiations refer to Figure 3-4.

At this point the designer has two choices: he can declare the internal assembly functions of AdderG at the type level or he can create different version instances of AdderSliceG and then declare and instantiate the internal assembly of AdderG. The second alternative is essentially a bottom-up approach that first tries to completely define the constituents of a design. In this example, we shall illustrate the second alternative.

In order to define versions of AdderSlice, the designer defines a type object that represents an internal assembly of the object:

User-Type : *adderslicewb1* subtype of *adderslicebb*;

It should be recalled that a type representing the internal assembly of an object (i.e., white-box object type) must be a subtype of the object that represents its external features (i.e., black-box object type).

This composite object references other objects HalfAdder and OR-gate, which must now be declared.

User-Type: *halfadderbb, orgatebb*;

Functions on these types can be defined as follows:

function ORName (*orgatebb*) $\rightarrow$ *charstring* u

function ORInput (*orgatebb*) $\rightarrow$ *terminal* m

function OROutput (*orgatebb*) $\rightarrow$ *terminal* u

function HName (*halfadderbb*) $\rightarrow$ *charstring* u

function HInput (*halfadderbb*) $\rightarrow$ *terminal* m

function HOutput (*halfadderbb*) $\rightarrow$ *terminal* m

{ ORName, HName } $\in D_S{}^1$

{ ORInput, OROutput, HInput, HOutput } $\in I_F$

The following instances of these types are created.

AddInstance HalfAdderG to type *halfadderbb*;

AddInstance AhalfAdderG to type *Generic*;

AddInstance OR-gateG to type *orgatebb*;

AddInstance OR-gateG to type *Generic*;

These functions for OR-gate and Halfadder are instantiated.

ORName (OR-gateG) := "OR-Gate";

ORInput (OR-gateG) := { I1, I2 };

OROutput (OR-gateG) := J ;

HName (HalfAdderG) := "Half-Adder1";

HInput (HalfAdderG) := { A1, B1 };

HOutput (HalfAdderG) := { S1, C1 };

The above declarations completes the descriptions of the external features of the component objects of AdderG. The designer can now build its internal assembly.

The functions — which represent the internal assembly — defined on the type *adderslicewb1* (a subtype of *adderslicebb*) are the following:

function ASConnect1 (*adderslicewb1, halfadderbb, halfadderbb*)

$\rightarrow$ <*terminal, terminal*>

function ASConnect2 (*adderslicewb1, halfadderbb, orgatebb*)

$\rightarrow$ <*terminal, terminal*>

function ASLink1 (*adderslicewb1, terminal*) $\rightarrow$ $<halfadderbb, terminal>$

function ASLink2 (*adderslicewb1, terminal*) $\rightarrow$ $<orgatebb, terminal>$

{ ASConnect1, ASConnect2, ASLink1, ASLink2 } $\in$ *IA*

Given all these types, instances, functions and function instances, the designer can create a version instance for AdderSliceG, which will have all the information needed to instantiate it. For this purpose, the operation *Create* (defined in Section 4.2.2) can be used.

Create instance of type *adderslicewb1* version of AdderSliceG;

This creates a new object which is an instance of *adderslicewb1*; it is also given the system-defined type *Versioned*. AdderSliceG is its generic object; thus, it value-acquires all the results of functions defined on this object and declared as either I_F or $D_S{}^1$. It should be recalled the user-defined type *adderslicebb* of the given generic object AdderSliceG is a supertype of *adderslicewb1*. Let the surrogate of the instance returned by this operation be Adderslice.V1. The *system* will update the following functions. "(S)" signifies action taken by the system.

GenericInst(Adderslice.V1) := AdderSliceG;   (S)

FirstVersion(AdderSliceG) := AdderSlice.V1;   (S)

InitialVersions(AdderSliceG) := { AdderSlice.V1};   (S)

VersionSet(AdderSliceG) := { AdderSlice.V1};   (S)

VersionNumber(AdderSlice.V1) := 1;   (S)

CreationTime(AdderSlice.V1) := 11/28/1989;   (S)

VersionStatus(AdderSlice.V1) := *Transient*;   (S)

Also by virtue of value-acquisition, the following results will be returned by the functions inherited by AdderSlivce.V1.

ASName (AdderSlice.V1) := "Adder-Slice";

ASInput (AdderSlice.V1) := { X, Y, CI };

ASOutput (AdderSlice.V1) := { Z, CO };

It should be recalled that AdderSlice.V1 inherits the function Designer from its generic object, but this is categorized as noninvariant D_S^2; thus, it can be updated at the version level.

Designer(AdderSlice.V1) := "Ostrominsky";

In order to fully describe the internal assembly of AdderSlice.V1, the designer will need the version instances of HalfAdderG. Thus, a version of HalfAdderG is created on the similar lines as shown for the case of AdderSliceG.

User-Type: *halfadderwb1* subtype of *halfadderbb*;

User-Type: *xorgatebb, andgatebb*

Following functions are defined on *halfadderwb1*.

function HContains (*halfadderwb1*) $\rightarrow$ <*xorgatebb, andgatebb*>

function HLink1 (*halfadderwb1, terminal*) $\rightarrow$ <*xorgatebb, terminal*> m

function HLink2 (*halfadderwb1, terminal*) $\rightarrow$ <*andgatebb, terminal*> m

It should be noted that this internal assembly does not have interconnection properties.

Create instance of type *halfadderwb1* version of HalfadderG;

Create instance of type *halfadderwb1* version of HalfadderG;

These creates a new object which is an instance of *halfadderwb1*; it is also given the system-defined type *Versioned*. HalfAdderG is its generic object; thus, it value-acquires all the results of functions defined on this object and declared as either I_F or $D_S{}^1$. The *system* updates the following functions.

GenericInst(Halfadder.V1) := HalfadderG;   (S)

FirstVersion(HalfadderG) := Halfadder.V1;   (S)

InitialVersions(HalfadderG) := { Halfadder.V1};   (S)

VersionSet(HalfadderG) := { Halfadder.V1};   (S)

VersionNumber(Halfadder.V1) := 1;   (S)

CreationTime(Halfadder.V1) := 11/29/1989;   (S)

VersionStatus(Halfadder.V1) := *Transient*;   (S)

We can create instances of XOR-gate and AND-gate and define the internal assembly of Halfadder.V1.

AddInstance XOR-gateG to type *xorgatebb*;

AddInstance XOR-gateG to type *Generic*;

AddInstance AND-gateG to type *andgatebb*;

AddInstance AND-gateG to type *Generic*;

The Halfadder.V1 is created in transient state. Therefore, a designer can make any update to its internal assembly. These internal assembly functions are instantiated below.

HContains (Halfadder.V1) := <XOR-gateG, AND-gateG>

HLink1 (Halfadder.V1, A) := <XOR-gateG, XO1>

HLink1 (Halfadder.V1, B) := <XOR-gateG, XO2>

HLink1 (Halfadder.V1, S1) := <XOR-gateG, XO3>

HLink2 (Halfadder.V1, A) := <AND-gateG, AN1>

HLink2 (Halfadder.V1, B) := <AND-gateG, AN2>

HLink2 (Halfadder.V1, C1) := <AND-gateG, AN3>

The above instantiations of functions HContain, HLink1, and HLink2 completely describe the internal assembly of Halfadder.V1. The reference to to its constituents are generic. It should be noted that generic reference is possible because of the concepts of interface attributes and value-acquisition. This idea of generic reference is extremely important, as it allows a designer to define composite objects without any concern about the internal structures of its constituents, which may be designed by other designers.

This version can be promoted to *stable* status and later the generic references can be modified to specific references (i.e., references to actual versions) under the rule of equivalence modification. To change its status, the operation *promote* can be used.

promote Halfadder.V1;

This changes the transient state of the given version into the stable state. Since Halfadder.V1 is a *stable* version, other versions can be derived from it. For deriving a new version from a given version, the operation *derive* (defined in Section 4.2.2) can be used.

derive from Halfadder.V1;

Let the surrogate of the version returned by the above operation be Halfadder.V2. As explained in Section 4.2.2, Halfadder.V2 is of the same user-defined type as Halfadder.V1. It also value-acquires all the invariant attributes from HalfadderG, the generic object of Halfadder.V1. It has identical external features and internal assembly as Halfadder.V1. Both Halfadder.V1 and Halfadder.V2 share their constituents AND-gateG and XOR-gateG as governed by Rule 4.1.

The values of system-defined functions are shown below.

GenericInst(Halfadder.V2) := HalfadderG;   (S)

VersionSet(HalfadderG) := { Halfadder.V1, Halfadder.V2 };   (S)

VersionNumber(Halfadder.V2) := 2;   (S)

CreationTime(Halfadder.V2) := 12/01/1989;   (S)

VersionStatus(Halfadder.V2) := *Transient*;   (S)

ImmedSuccessor (Halfadder.V1) := Halfadder.V2;   (S)

These functions show the relationships among the generic object HalfadderG and its two versions. It should be noted that VersionNumber is the identifier assigned by the system, which is unique within a version set. The user-given identifier to the generic object (and value-acquired by its versions) and system-assigned VersionNumber can uniquely identify any versioned object. The references to surrogate as used in this example are not mandatory.

Halfadder.V2 starts in the transient state and after some modifications, it can be promoted to the stable status.

At this point, a designer has all the constituent objects needed to define the internal assembly of AdderSlice.V1. It can be done by the following instantiations.

ASContains (AdderSlice.V1) := < Halfadder.V1, Halfadder.V2, OR-gateG >;

ASConnect1 (AdderSlice.V1, Halfadder.V1, Halfadder.V2) :=   < S1, B1 >;

ASConnect2 (AdderSlice.V1, Halfadder.V1, OR-gateG) :=   < C1, I1 >;

ASConnect2 (AdderSlice.V1, Halfadder.V2, OR-gateG) :=   < C1, I2 >;

ASLink1 (AdderSlice.V1, X) :=   < HalfAdder.V1, A1 >;

ASLink1 (AdderSlice.V1, Y) :=   < HalfAdder.V1, B1 >;

ASLink1 (AdderSlice.V1, CI) :=   < HalfAdder.V2, A1 >;

ASLink1 (AdderSlice.V1, Z) := < Halfadder.V2, S1 >;

ASLink2 (AdderSlice.V1, CO) := < OR-gateG, J >;

These functions completely describe the internal assembly of AdderSlice.V1. It should be noted that it makes specific references to HalfAdders but a generic reference to OR-gate. This generic referenced can be dereferenced to any version instance of OR-gateG that is designated as the default version.

AdderSlice.V1 can be promoted to the stable status.

promote AdderSlice.V1;

AdderSlice.V1 is a stable version; it cannot be updated but for equivalence modification and changes in its $D_S{}^2$ attributes that are categorized as *nonversion-significant*. For instance, we can update its Designer function.

Designer (AdderSlice.V1) := "Chang";

However, its internal assembly, being version-significant, cannot be modified in the stable state. If the designer wants to experiment with an entirely different version, he needs to create a new version from the generic object AdderSliceG. (In this example, this new version corresponds to Figure 3-6.) It is done by the following declarations.

User-Type: *adderslicewb2* subtype of *adderslicebb*;

New functions can be defined on this type.

function ASNContains(*adderslicewb2)* →
< *xorgatebb, xorgatebb, orgatebb, andgatebb, andgatebb, andgatebb* >;
function ASNConnect1 (*adderslicewb2, xorgatebb, xorgatebb*) →
< *terminal, terminal*>;
function ASNConnect2 (*adderslicewb2, orgatebb, andgatebb*) →

$<terminal,\ terminal>$;

function ASNLink1 ($adderslicewb2,\ andgatebb$) $\rightarrow$ $<terminal,\ terminal>$;

function ASNLink2 ($adderslicewb2,\ xorgatebb$) $\rightarrow$ $<terminal,\ terminal>$;

function ASNLink3 ($adderslicewb2,\ orgatebb$) $\rightarrow$ $<terminal,\ terminal>$;

{ ASNContain, ASNConnect1, ASNConnect2, ASNLink1, ASNLink2,

ASNLink3 } $\in$ IA

A new version of this type can be created by the following command:

Create instance of type $adderslicewb2$ version of AdderSliceG;

Let the surrogate of the versioned object returned by this operation be AdderSlice.V2. The system updates the following functions:

GenericInst(Adderslice.V2) := AdderSliceG;　　　　　　　　(S)

InitialVersions(AdderSliceG) := { AdderSlice.V1, AdderSlice.V2};　(S)

VersionSet(AdderSliceG) := { AdderSlice.V1, AdderSlice.V2};　　(S)

VersionNumber(AdderSlice.V2) := 2;　　　　　　　　　　(S)

CreationTime(AdderSlice.V2) := 12/13/1989;　　　　　　　(S)

VersionStatus(AdderSlice.V2) := $Transient$;　　　　　(S)

Also by virtue of value-acquisition, the following results will be returned by the functions inherited by AdderSlice.V2:

ASName (AdderSlice.V2)　:= "Adder-Slice";

ASInput (AdderSlice.V2)　:= { X, Y, CI };

ASOutput (AdderSlice.V2)　:= { Z, CO };

The next step would be to define the internal structure of the highest level (for the purpose of this example) object AdderG, as it has its components and their versions completely defined. However, we stop our example at this point.

We have illustrated some of the important aspects of the methodology developed for version control and management in Chapter 4. In the example given here, the details of function declarations and instantiations were perhaps a little distracting. However, these details were necessary, as we chose a well-understood real-world object for this example. This showed the validity and the usefulness of the proposed methodology for versioning.

REFERENCES

[Agr89] Agrawal, R., Borgida, A., and Jagadish, H. V., "Efficient Management of Transitive Relationships in Large Data and Knowledge Bases," *Proc. ACM-SIGMOD Conf.*, Portland, OR (1989).

[Bat84] Batory, D. S., and Buchmann, A. P., "Molecular Objects, Abstract Data Types, and Data Models - A Framework," *Proc. VLDB Conf.*, Singapore (1984).

[Bat85] Batory, D. S., and Kim, W.,"Modeling Concepts for VLSI CAD Objects," *ACM TODS*, vol. 10, no. 3, p. 322-346 (1985).

[Bee88] Beech, D. and Mahbod, B., "Generalized Version Control in an Object-Oriented Database," *IEEE Conf. on Data Engineering,*, Los Angeles, CA (1988).

[Ben82] Bennet, J., "A Database Management System for Design Engineers," *19th Design Automation Conf.*, New York, NY (1982).

[Buc85] Buchmann, A. P., and Celis, C. P., "An Architecture and Data Model for CAD databases," *Proc. VLDB Conf.*, Stockholm, Sweden (1985).

[Car86] Carey, M. J., DeWitt, D. J., Richardson, J. E., and Shekita, E. J., "Object and File Management in the EXODUS Extensible Database System," *Proc. VLDB Conf.*, Kyoto, Japan (1986).

[Cho86] Chou, H-T. and Kim, W., "A Unifying Framework for Version Control in a CAD Environment," *Proc. VLDB Conf.*, Kyoto, Japan (1986).

[Eas80] Eastman, C. M., "System Facilities for CAD Databases," *Proc. Design Automation Conf.*, Washington, D,C. (1980).

[Emo83] Emond, J. C., and Marechal, G., "A computer Aided-Design System Based On A Relational DBMS," *ACM SIGMOD/IEEE Engineering Design Applications*, Atlanta, GA (1983).

[Fis87] Fishman, D. H., "Iris: An Object-Oriented Database Management System," *ACM TOOIS,* vol. 5, no. 1, p. 48-69 (1987).

[Got86] Goto, S., "*Advances in CAD: Design Methodologies,*" North-Holland, New York, NY (1986).

[Har87] Harder, T., Meyer-Wegner, K., Mitschang, B., and Sikeler, A., "PRIMA, A DBMS Prototype Supporting Engineering Applications," *Proc. VLDB Conf.*, Brighton, U. K. (1987).

124

[Ioa88]   Ioannidis, Y. E., and Ramakrishnan, R., "On the Computation of the Transitive Closure Algorithm," *Proc. VLDB Conf.*, Los Angeles, CA (1988).

[Jag88]   Jagadish, H. V., "A Compressed Transitive Closure Technique for Efficient Fixed-Point Query System," *Proc. Expert Database Systems*, Tysons Corner, Virginia (1988).

[Joh83]   Johnson, H. R., and Schweitzer, J. E., "A DBMS facilities for Handling Structured Enginnering Entities," *ACM/IEEE Engineering Design Aplications*, Atlanta, GA (1983).

[Kat82]   Katz, R. H., "A Database Approach for Managing VLSI Design Data," *Proc. of 19th Design Automation Conf.*, Las Vegas (1982).

[Kat85]   Katz, R. H., *Information Management for Engineering Design,*, Springer-Verlag, New York, NY (1985).

[Kat86]   Katz, R., Chang, E., and Bhateja, R., "Version Modeling Concepts for Computer-Aided Design Databases," *Proc. ACM SIGMOD Conf.*, Washington, D. C. (1986).

[Ket88a]   Ketabchi, M. A., and Berzins, V., "An Object-Oriented Semantic Data Model for CAD Applications," *Information Sciences*, vol. 46, no. 1, p. 109-139 (1988)

[Ket88b]   Ketabchi, M. A., and Berzins, V., "Mathematical Model of Composite Objects and Its Application for Organizing Engineering Databases," *IEEE Trans. on Software Engineering*, vol. 14, no. 1, p. 71-84 (1988).

[Kim87]   Kim, W., Chou, H-T., and Banerjee, J., "Operations and Implementation of Complex Objects," *Proc. of Data Engineering Conf.*, Los Angeles, CA (1987).

[Kim89]   Kim, W., Bertino, E., and Garza, J. F., "Composite Object Support Revisited," *Proc. ACM-SIGMOD Conf.*, Portland, OR (1989).

[Kla86]   Klahold, P. and Schlageter, G., "A General Model for Version Management in Databases," Proc. of VLDB Conf., Kyoto, Japan (1986).

[Lan86]   Landis, G. S., "Design Evolution and History in an Object-Oriented CAD/CAM Database," *IEEE COMPCON*, San Francisco, CA (1986).

[Lor82]   Lorie, R. A., "Issues in Databases for Design Applications," *File Structures and Databases for CAD, IFIP*, Columbus, OH (1982).

[Lor83]   Lorie, R. A., and Plouffe, W., "Complex Objects and Their Use in Design Transactions," *ACM SIGMOD/IEEE Engineering Design Applications*, San Jose, CA (1983).

126

[McL83]   McLeod, D. and Rao, K. V., "An Approach to Information Management for CAD/VLSI Applications," *ACM SIGMOD/IEEE, Engineering Design Applications*, San Jose, CA (1983).

[Mei83]   Meier, A., and Lorie, R. A., "A Surrogate Concept for Enginnering Databases," *Proc. of VLDB Conf.*, Venice, Italy (1983).

[Nav88]   Navathe, S. B., and Ahmed, R., "Temporal Aspects of Version Management," *IEEE Data Engineering Special Issue*, vol. 11, no. 4, p. 34-37 (1988).

[Neu83]   Neumann, T., "On Representing the Design Information in a Common Database," *ACM/IEE Engineering Design Applications*, San Jose, CA (1983).

[Rob81]   Roberts, K. A., Baker, T. E., and Jerome, D. H., "A Vertically Organized Computer-Aided Design Database," *Proc. 18th Design Automation Conf.*, Boston, MA (1981).

[Sch77]   Schkolnick, M., "A Clustering Algorithm for Hierarchical Structures," *ACM Trans. on Database Systems*, vol. 2, no. 1, p. 27-44 (1977).

[Sch83]   Schubert, M. A., Papalaskaris, M. A., and Taugher, J., "Determining Type, Part, Color and Time Relationships," *IEEE Computer*, vol. 16, no. 10, p. 53-61 (1983).

[Sto83]   Stonebraker, M., Rubenstein, B., and Guttman, A., "Application of Abstract Data Types and Abstract Indices to CAD Databases," *ACM SIGMOD/IEEE Engineering Design Applications*, San Jose, CA (1983).

[Su88]   Su, S. Y. W., Krishnamurthy, V., and Lam, H., "An Object-Oriented Semantic Association Model (OSAM*)," *AI in Industrial and Manufacturing: Theoretical Issues and Applications*, S. Kumara, R. L. Kashyap, and A. L. Soyster (Eds.), American Institute of Industrial Engineers, New York, NY (1988).

[Wie82]   Wiederhold, G., Beetam, A. F., and Short, G. E., "A Database Approach to Communication in VLSI Design," *IEEE Trans. on CAD of ICS*, vol 1, no. 2, p. 35-38 (1982).

BIOGRAPHICAL SKETCH

Given a choice, Rafi Ahmed would leave this page blank to signify the inanity of life. But this biographical sketch, being a categorical imperative, follows.

He was born in Muzaffarpur, India, where he studied mathematics and found solace in logical empiricism. At the University of Florida, he got a master's degree in computer and information sciences. In the years that followed, he pursued his doctoral degree while spending his time in research, teaching and working with the industry.

He likes computers, computation, classical music, chess, tennis and the rational explanation of this universe.

I certify that I have read this study and that in my opinion it conforms to acceptable standards of scholarly presentation and is fully adequate, in scope and quality, as a dissertation for the degree of Doctor of Philosophy.

Shamkant B. Navathe, Chairman
Professor of Computer and Information Sciences

I certify that I have read this study and that in my opinion it conforms to acceptable standards of scholarly presentation and is fully adequate, in scope and quality, as a dissertation for the degree of Doctor of Philosophy.

Stanley Y. W. Su
Professor of Computer and Information Sciences

I certify that I have read this study and that in my opinion it conforms to acceptable standards of scholarly presentation and is fully adequate, in scope and quality, as a dissertation for the degree of Doctor of Philosophy.

Sharma Chakravarthy
Associate Professor of Computer and Information Sciences

I certify that I have read this study and that in my opinion it conforms to acceptable standards of scholarly presentation and is fully adequate, in scope and quality, as a dissertation for the degree of Doctor of Philosophy.

Prabhat Hajela
Associate Professor of Aerospace Engineering, Mechanics, and Engineering Sciences

I certify that I have read this study and that in my opinion it conforms to acceptable standards of scholarly presentation and is fully adequate, in scope and quality, as a dissertation for the degree of Doctor of Philosophy.

Ravi Varadarajan
Assistant Professor of Computer and Information Sciences

This dissertation was submitted to the Graduate Faculty of the College of Engineering and to the Graduate School and was accepted for partial fulfillment of the requirements of the degree of Doctor of Philosophy.

December 1989

for Winfred M. Phillips
Dean, College of Engineering

Madelyn M. Lockhart
Dean, Graduate School